THE
COMPU
PRIM

50p

THE COMPUTER PRIMER

FELIX REDMILL

British Telecom International

ADDISON-WESLEY PUBLISHING COMPANY

Wokingham, England · Reading, Massachusetts · Menlo Park, California
Don Mills, Ontario · Amsterdam · Sydney · Bonn · Singapore
Tokyo · Madrid · Bogota · Santiago · San Juan

Cover by Crayon Design, Henley-on-Thames.
Cover photography by Michael Taylor.
Typeset by Columns, Reading.
Printed in Great Britain by Billing & Sons Ltd, Worcester.

British Library Cataloguing in Publication Data

Redmill, Felix
The computer primer.
1. Electronic digital computers
I. Title
004 QA76.5

ISBN 0–201–18058–8

Library of Congress Cataloging in Publication Data

Redmill, Felix
The computer primer.

Includes index.
1. Electronic data processing. 2. Computers.
I. Title.
QA76.R39 1987 004 86–28878
ISBN 0–201–18058–8

ABCDEFG 893210987

To
my mother
and
my friends in St Kitts

Acknowledgement

While this book was being written, extracts from Part II were used as the basis of a series of articles published in the *Far Eastern Technical Review*. Acknowledgement is made to the editor.

At the same time, an introductory briefing course on computers was also based on Part II. This provided an opportunity for a critical review of the structure and content of that part of the book and the author wishes to thank the International Telecommunication Union for its sponsorship.

Preface

This book is written for all who wish a sound briefing on information technology and computers without taking too much time about it. It does not assume prior knowledge of the subject, but nor does it avoid detail. It particularly addresses business and professional users since their involvement with computers, although already substantial, is increasing rapidly. Not only are they using information technology in their decision making processes, but they are frequently having to make decisions on where, when and how best to employ computers. This book is intended to provide the understanding of the subject necessary for such decisions.

Part I offers an introduction to information technology. Not only does it discuss the microcomputer and its applications but also networks. Further, Chapter 4 describes the stages of a computer installation project and Chapter 5 provides extensive advice on how to go about purchasing a microcomputer system. It is hoped that these two chapters will prove valuable to anyone involved in these activities, even the computer-literate.

Part II presents the fundamentals of computers. Readers may treat it as an easy-to-read course in the subject or as a reference source to be dipped into when information is needed.

Part III discusses the trends in computing which are expected to culminate in the so-called fifth generation computers of the 1990s.

Finally, the Glossary provides a further reference source. It has not been restricted to terms used in this book and may therefore be found useful as a more general dictionary of expressions used in information technology.

CONTENTS

PART I

COMPUTERS AND THE MANAGER

A briefing in information technology and advice on introducing a computer system, whether by development project or purchase. Computer literacy is not generally assumed in Part I, but terms may be used without explanation if they are defined in Part II or in the Glossary.

CHAPTER 1

INFORMATION TECHNOLOGY AND THE MANAGER

Until recently, computers were regarded with a certain awe. They have never been anything more than processors of information, but their newness and high cost, and the consequent lack of an understanding of them, kept them at arm's length from the general public and surrounded them with mystique.

With the development of the microprocessor a rapid change took place. The public were brought closer to the technology. They learned that such familiar domestic appliances as washing machines were now microprocessor controlled. Then the microcomputer, or micro, became available at a price which allowed the public at large to become not only computer users but, indeed, computer owners. Many such owners were content to use their machines to run only pre-written software, often in the form of games. Many others, however, wanted to apply their computers to practical needs, to experiment and to write programs. Since then the microcomputer has become commonplace in both the business world and the home and dependence on it has grown in all areas of industry and commerce.

Meanwhile the field of information technology has evolved out of the convergence of computing and communications. The microcomputer has become more than a mere processing tool; it is now the hub of office facilities and the gateway to both data and computer-based services.

INFORMATION TECHNOLOGY

With the miniaturization of processors, the ready availability of microcomputers, the proliferation of computer technology and, above all, the integration of computers and communications – i.e. the integration of information processing with information access and transfer – the attitude to the relationship between the computer and the information it processes has altered: the information is recognized as being the subject of importance and the computer merely the tool for handling it. This is not to say that the computer is trivial or any less important than hitherto; it is a most sophisticated tool. Nevertheless, as the computer has increased its hold and its power over us – for how could we now exist without it? – so, paradoxically, its exposure and familiarity have induced us, to a large extent, to shed our great awe of it. At the same time, the computer has assisted in this transfer of priority by making information more readily available, more easily processed, more easily and cheaply communicated, and therefore more demanding of attention. Thus has **information technology** (IT) become a subject of major importance.

In the early years, computers received data almost exclusively from manual inputs via paper tape and punched cards. During the 1960s the demand for communication between computers grew, and this was satisfied by **modems** which converted a computer's digital data into an analogue form suitable for transmission over the **public switched telephone network** (PSTN). In the 1970s, however, digital networks became available and these not only facilitated intercomputer communication, but also encouraged and enabled it to grow. They allowed computers not only to dispatch data to each other but also, given the right software, to access a central database or each other's databases. Banking and airline systems were notable exponents of **remote access** of databases. And methods of using networks to best advantage were evolving: it was possible for local computers to store the data most relevant to their needs and still have access to other databases via communication systems and special software. Developments in communications were serving the needs of computers.

Meanwhile, computers were serving communications. The

control systems of telephone exchanges, consisting of purely logical processes, had been early choices for computerization and a new generation of public exchanges and **private automatic branch exchanges** (PABXs) was rapidly replacing the obsolescent analogue equipment. The computerized PABXs offered miniaturization, speed of operation, cheapness, and a number of automatic facilities such as short code dialling, three-party calls, and call transfer under a number of conditions.

The digital networks, mentioned above, also owed their existence to computers and computer technology. Indeed, telecommunications has entered an era based primarily on computers. At the same time the huge expansion in the use of computers is founded on the new telecommunications equipment and techniques. It is the merging of these two technologies which has been the foundation of information technology and which has placed information in the pre-eminent position which it now enjoys. Automatic data collection, seemingly inexhaustible storage, easy and rapid retrieval and updating of data and fast transmission combine to create an environment conducive to the expectation of information being available on demand. Decisions are facilitated; and the need is created for further decisions concerning the management of information.

THE WORD PROCESSOR

While technology was evolving to facilitate information processing in general, software was being written to allow computers to provide new facilities to the business community. Perhaps the most far reaching of these, and the one which is the foundation of computerizing the office, is the electronic typewriter or word processor.

The word processor is a microcomputer with software which carries out text processing. Inputs to it are from a typist's keyboard and these are in the form of text to be processed and instructions as to what form processing should take. In short, the forms of processing cover all the operations which a secretary may wish to carry out on text. Outputs are to a visual display unit, for monitoring by the typist, and a printer for a hard copy.

The input text is stored in computer memory and is therefore easily changed from the keyboard. Bulk storage, for permanent storage of documents, is provided by floppy disks. Text can therefore be stored, corrected, displayed and printed at will. Also, since word processing is controlled by computers and communication between computers is possible, communication between word processors is available. Information input in one place can immediately be transmitted electronically to another, stored in electronic memory, displayed on a terminal screen, and produced as hard copy on a printer.

Word processors also provide other conveniences. Being computers, their memories can be used to store standard letters and circulars which may be printed and dispatched under given circumstances. They can store lists of names and addresses which may be applied, at a single command, to make each copy of an outgoing circular personally addressed to the recipient. This facility is now extensively used, not only in offices, but by advertising departments.

The first word processors were designed only for word processing. Although they were computers, they did not contain operating systems to allow their more general application. They lacked the flexibility which the integration of word processing with other computer uses could provide. So word processing software packages, for use on general-purpose microcomputers, arrived on the market. These are gaining in popularity and, as long as the computer on which they are used is provided with an adequate display unit and a fast printer, they are as good as the dedicated word processors – and they offer the added flexibility of combining word processing with data processing.

THE ELECTRONIC OFFICE

One of the most prolific users of information is the manager. It is not surprising, therefore, that a significant amount of effort has been devoted to applying information technology to the automation of the office. Consequently the secretary's and manager's offices are rapidly becoming computerized. The individual functions are being not only automated but also integrated and this in turn facilitates the transfer and multiple use of information.

While the secretary has replaced the typewriter with a word processor, the manager is using a microcomputer to store and process information and various software packages to analyse data and display results. If the manager's computer is connected to the secretary's, these results can be transmitted between machines, used by the word processing package and incorporated in documents or letters prepared by the secretary.

Within businesses, **local area networks** (LANs – see Chapter 3) are being used to link the microcomputers in managers' officers. These allow the transmission of messages (electronic mail) between terminals. Such networks are usually hosted on a larger (usually a mini) computer which provides other conveniences, such as long term storage of all mail sent, stored telephone directories, and calculating machine facilities.

In addition, software packages are being developed for specific purposes, such as project management, and these are run by managers on their microcomputers, or even on portable computers for use at home or on journeys. Work prepared on these can be transferred to larger machines in the office for integration with other work, faster processing, better resolution of graphical output, better and faster printing, etc.

The office is placing increasing reliance on the computer – and on computer-based communications, for computers not only provide the control for modern communications networks but they also process the information sent over them. Thus, Chapter 3 discusses the subject of networks.

Applications Software

Computer users fall into different classes, each requiring the computer system for a different purpose. Scientists need to solve mathematical problems, industrialists need computers to control manufacturing and service processes, businesses demand the storage and frequent updating of extensive filing systems, and home computer users want to play games. The programs which are written, bought or borrowed by users to orchestrate their computers to perform these functions are the **applications programs.**

A large proportion of applications programs are written or commissioned by users for single applications, since many users' problems are in some way unique. However, there are problems common to many users and there is a wide range of facilities which, if offered on computers, would be extensively used. Programs written to solve such problems or provide such facilities are becoming increasingly plentiful as pre-written applications software packages, and many of these have huge potential markets.

Indeed, the miniaturization, cost reduction, and consequent proliferation of microcomputers have introduced the computer to new categories of user and have created an almost insatiable market for pre-written applications software. An increasing number of facility programs are therefore becoming available as proprietary items, or **packages**. The range of applications of these packages is already wide and expanding. For example, educational packages offer instruction in diverse fields, from learning a foreign language to flying an aircraft; games provide ready, and sometimes expensive, diversion; and business packages furnish businessmen with quick results to repetitive problems, as well as a legitimate excuse to play with a computer. Then there are the packages which have applications in a wide and general field. For example, 'spelling checkers' store a vocabulary of words against which the words in a document or letter are compared; discrepancies are highlighted so that the typist is guided to where changes may be required.

SPREADSHEETS

Probably the best selling and most widely used of all applications packages are **spreadsheets**. These are general purpose, and are designed for the storage of data and its presentation in a tabular, and sometimes graphical form, but are extensively used for financial planning. These programs have three aspects: the formatted screen presentation from which they derive their name, the creation of a database where they store input data and results, and logic for carrying out calculations. They provide the flexibility for a user to define the data presentation, inserting column and row headings, and to input the formulae for carrying out calculations. They then store these requirements.

In operation spreadsheets present, on the screen, the user's defined and labelled matrix into which the user inserts data, via the keyboard and guided by a **cursor** on the screen. As this is done, the position into which each item of data is placed on the screen is interpreted by the program to determine where in the database it should be stored. As soon as the required amount of data has been entered, the program automatically calculates results, by applying the user's formulae, and displays them in the appropriate positions in the matrix on the screen.

In this way, the program provides a model which rapidly and easily tests a chosen set of assumptions and displays the results. It can then be used to test a different set of assumptions. One application of spreadsheets is in budget planning where they offer a fast and automated comparison of strategic or tactical options.

A simple spreadsheet example is given in Figure 1.1. This shows the spreadsheet as an 8×8 matrix with the rows labelled from 1 to 8 and the columns A to H. The matrix thus contains 64 'cells' and it is usually permissible to store a heading, a number or a formula in any cell. Thus, cells C2, D2, E2, F2 and G2, as well as A3, A4 and A5 contain headings. These are simply written in after positioning the screen cursor in the appropriate cell. Likewise, cells C3, C4, C5, D3, D4, D5, F3, F4 and F5 contain numbers (values) which are entered in the same way. However, although the cells in the E and G columns are seen to contain values, these are, in fact, not entered manually but are the results of calculations based on the values in the C, D and F columns. For example, the profit on ITEM 1 equals its Cost Price multiplied by its Percentage Mark Up. Thus, if the formula, C3 × D3/100, were entered into the cell E3, the value displayed in that cell would always be the result of this calculation, based on the contents of cells C3 and D3. Similarly, the sale price for each item may be displayed in the G column by entering the formula, (C3 + E3) × F3/100, in the appropriate cells. With these formulae in place, a salesman need only change the C and D column values in order to obtain an immediate display of the altered sale prices and profits. Comparisons of profit margins for different sale prices of the same item can easily be made, as can comparisons between different items, different brands, and so on.

Only the basis of the spreadsheet has been described and all spreadsheets have greater powers and wider applications

	A	B	C	D	E	F	G	H
1								
2			COST PRICE	MARK UP %	PROFIT	VAT RATE %	SALE PRICE	
3	ITEM 1		300	6	18	15	365.7	
4	ITEM 2		249	11	27.4	15	317.8	
5	ITEM 3		285	8	22.8	15	354	
6								
7								
8								

Figure 1.1 *Example of a spreadsheet as seen on a screen.*

than merely calculating costs. They are used for a huge variety of purposes.

SOFTWARE PACKAGES AND MICROS

While many applications packages are suitable for use on microcomputers, many require facilities which some micros may not possess. The first point to note is that all applications software must exist in, or be translated into, a machine language. They may therefore only be applicable to certain hardware.

The next point is that many packages depend on a certain operating system for their functioning. They are then only viable on computers which have that operating system. Typically, spreadsheets are available for use on micros, subject only to these software limitations.

However, there are other restrictions to the general compatibility of applications packages with micros. Some packages, such as database management systems, require large amounts of memory, which a micro may not be able to sustain. Further, some applications require their host computer to be able to accommodate a number of terminals, and many micros only possess a single input/output **port**. For example, there are a number of accounting packages available for storing and displaying a business' transactions and ledger files. If these files are to be kept up-to-date by inputting all transactions as they occur, it may be necessary for a number of persons, perhaps in different locations, all to have access to the computer from their own terminals. The requirement, in this case, is for a **multi-user** computer. This has a number of ports to allow the connection of several terminals, and an operating system which provides the internal organization for such a system. A large-scale example of a multi-user application is an airline booking system, in which a large number of terminals all have access to the same computer and the same database.

A further limitation on the use of micros for running applications packages is the quality of their peripherals. For example, there are a number of word processing packages on the market and running these on a micro offers advantages over using a dedicated word processor, since it allows the possibility of combining text handling with data processing. However, if the micro does not, or cannot, use a fast printer, only small jobs are possible and, in many cases, the advantage is negated or reduced.

Similarly, there are a number of **graphics packages** available for presenting various types of data in graphical form. These, however, are of little use unless the computer on which they are run can drive a high resolution display unit or a graph plotter. Their advantage is lost unless the correct peripheral is provided.

Thus, in purchasing software packages, the hardware requirements for their effective use must be considered; and, likewise, in selecting a computer, the software likely to be run on it should be determined in advance if possible. Indeed, the choice of a computer depends on a wide range of criteria and these are considered at greater length in Chapter 5.

CHAPTER 2
THE MICRO

For many years computers have been changing the ways in which businesses function. However, it has only been since the recent arrival of the microprocessor, that the manager's rôle has itself been revolutionized. Now the impact of the micro is being felt by managers in all types of business. Word processors have replaced typewriters everywhere. Small businessmen are increasingly automating their files using microcomputers. In larger businesses the electronic office is replacing traditional filing methods and introducing a wide range of new communications facilities. Moreover, the impact of the micro has not been confined to the office: its influence has been enormous in all fields of industry and commerce – and in the home.

But what *is* a micro?

FOUR GENERATIONS OF COMPUTER HARDWARE

The first electronic computers, in the 1940s, (now referred to as the first generation of computers), were based on valve technology. They were consequently enormous, a single computer occupying a couple of dozen large racks (or frames) of equipment. Because the average life of the valves in use was only about 10 000 hours, there had to be a trade-off between the reliability of the computer and its processing power. If the computer consisted of more than 10 000 valves, it was likely to have a **mean time between failures** (MTBF) of less than one hour.

In second generation computers, the valve was replaced

with the newly invented transistor. Size decreased and the greater reliability of the transistor eliminated the reliability *vs* processing power trade-off. Computers were still composed of discrete components.

In the 1960s, the development of the integrated circuit, in which electronic circuits comprising many components are etched onto a silicon chip, led to the third generation. Again there was a significant reduction in size (for the same processing power).

Following this, the integrated circuit was improved through **large scale integration** (LSI), in which up to about 20 000 components were contained on a chip, to **very large scale integration** (VLSI), in which a single silicon chip is host to up to 100 000 components. The latter gave rise, in the late 1970s and early 1980s, to the fourth generation of computers. Miniturization was increased to such an extent that the microcomputer as we know it became possible.

Not only was the computer's circuitry reduced in size, but so was its memory. In the second generation, **primary storage** had consisted of magnetic **core store** and, in the third generation, **semiconductor memory** began to supersede this. In the fourth generation, the changeover had occurred. Semiconductor memory was refined to the point where 64 **kilobytes** (Kbytes) could be housed on a chip. (Now, 256-Kbyte chips are available and improvements on this are at the design stage.) Internal memory was thus reducing in price and increasing in miniaturization.

THE MICRO

So, after all that, what is a micro? A microprocessor is a computer's **central processing unit** (CPU – see Part II) on a single chip. When internal memory is added to this, along with input and output circuitry and connections, a microcomputer is created, and this need only comprise a few chips.

With peripheral equipment also reduced in size and price, it is now possible to build a micro system of impressive capability, at relatively low cost. An example is shown in Figure 2.1 in which a microcomputer is **host** to a number of terminals, each of which may have its own printer. A graphics plotter, a floppy disk drive, a hard disk for greater bulk storage, and a magnetic tape drive complete the system. The micro itself may now contain up to about four megabytes (4 Mbytes) of primary storage and the disk storage shown in the figure can provide tens of megabytes.

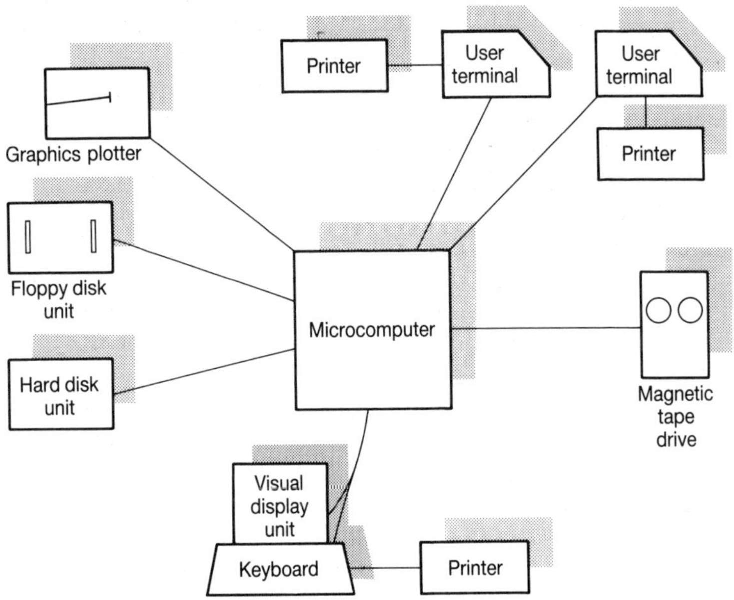

Figure 2.1 *System consisting of a microcomputer and various peripherals.*

Mainframe and Mini

Having briefly described the micro and its history, it is worth distinguishing it from mainframes and minis. However, it is also important to note that as miniaturization increases and micros become more powerful, the relative definitions of the three classes of computer are frequently changing. At the same time, the boundaries between the three classes are becoming increasingly blurred and distinctions between adjacent classes more difficult to specify.

Generally speaking, mainframes are defined by their capability. They are hugely powerful and their price reflects this. They are also physically large (by modern standards) and are capable of handling tens of **megabytes** (Mbytes) and even

gigabytes (Gbytes), of primary storage. Their **word length** is large – usually 32 or 64 bits (four or eight bytes), though machines designed for special purposes may have other word lengths. Mainframes can handle large numbers of peripherals and very large databases. A typical mainframe application is the support of an airline's booking system, in which terminals located all over a country need to access a single database.

Minicomputers are considerably smaller and cheaper than mainframes. Generally, they can perform similar functions, but on a smaller scale. Typically they contain up to 16 Mbytes of primary storage and have a word length of 32 bits. They are now being used in many businesses in applications which hitherto demanded mainframes, such as the handling of payroll systems. Their greater speed and larger **random access memory** (RAM) make them more suitable than micros for applications which need to handle very large amounts of data, particularly when structured databases are employed. The very largest databases, however, need the storage and power resources of a mainframe and it is only small systems which are suitable for use on microcomputers – and then only if the number of accesses of the database in a given time is limited.

A further distinction between the three classes of computers is their input/output capability. A mainframe can sustain a very large number (hundreds) of terminals. An example is an airline reservations system, in which the terminals in a large number of offices are connected to the same computer system. Minis can usually handle tens of terminals. Micros are often designed to handle a single terminal, though some can accommodate up to about ten. However, if all the terminals are in use concurrently, the response times can be very poor.

Having made these distinctions, it should be said that today's micros are as powerful and versatile as the minis of a few years ago. In another few years, the micros will have overtaken today's minis. Indeed, the next family of micros has a word length of 32 bits and the capability of handling 16 or more megabytes of random access memory (RAM).

APPLICATIONS OF MICROS

The takeover of office functions by microcomputers and microprocessor controlled devices has been discussed, but the range of applications of the micro is considerably wider than this. It would not be possible to provide an exhaustive list, but some typical examples might be helpful.

First there are the microprocessor control applications in which the extra storage and full input/output facilities of a computer are not required. These include the control of many domestic appliances, such as washing machines. The control of fuel injection, the ignition system and the instrumentation of motor vehicles is another example. A further example, but one in which some input is required, is in the monitoring of petrol flow in petrol pumps. Here inputs are necessary at times of price changes. Further illustrations of such applications, in which monitoring and display are the prominent features, are lift and cash register control. In these, limited ranges of external inputs form the data to be processed.

Then there are the microcomputers which are put to a specific and limited use. With the micros themselves being freely available, an increasing number of software packages are being written (and sold) for their application to tasks which are common to certain types of organization. For example, there are programs which make use of databases to provide storage and control of a medical General Practitioner's patient list. Equivalent packages offer office facilities of the type used by accountants and solicitors. Within this category of application comes **computer aided learning** (CAL). Here, programs written for self-tuition in numerous subjects are used in a wide range of teaching institutions, from universities to primary schools. Not only do these packages provide information, but they question the student on it. By comparing the student's answer, input at the keyboard, with the correct answer (and likely incorrect answers), stored in the machine, the program is able to deduce what response to make to the student.

There are, of course, the applications in which the microcomputer is used for running application programs writter by the user. The range of uses of this type is enormous, from amateur home users, through small office tasks, to the projects of university students and, ultimately to database, real-time and on-line applications (see below) which extend the micros to the full extent of their resources.

As final examples of uses to which micros are being put, the fields of **computer aided design** (CAD) and **computer aided**

manufacture (CAM) are important. CAD is a powerful tool which is already the recognized foundation of a designer's office. It is based on a model of the design being stored in the computer, its high resolution graphical presentation on a screen, and the ability of the designer to interact with the model, using the graphical representation as the input medium. Thus the designer creates a database to store the design model. He may also need mathematical programs to solve the equations necessary to calculate the design parameters. He then has the ability to segment the design model so that small modules of it can be displayed on the screen by a graphics package. He requires from the graphics package the ability of applying tests to the design model by interacting with the screen representation via a **light pen**, **mouse**, or **keyboard cursor**. Finally, when the designer makes alterations to the model, these must be rapidly reflected in the screen representation.

Clearly a full CAD system is the integration of a number of software tools, from database management systems to interactive graphics. Its wide range of potential applications and already extensive use are examples of the influence of IT on the field of engineering. Interestingly, one of the earliest and most extensive users of CAD has been the IT industry itself: more than 90% of all very large scale integrated (VLSI) circuitry is designed using CAD.

CAM too has advanced in recent years. Manufacturing, being a step-by-step repetitive process – as can be witnessed on any production line, is an ideal candidate for computerization. Many such processes – such as assembly and spray painting – require a fair degree of precision, and this is ensured when automation is by processor controlled machines, or robots. Many production lines, for example in the motor industry, are now operated in this way.

Process control is also becoming more widespread – for example, in the manufacture of chemicals. The principle is that a computer controls a sequence of operations, from the input of fixed quantities of raw materials, through the monitoring and control of environmental conditions, such as temperature and pressure, to the output of the finished product.

The gap between CAD and CAM is becoming smaller as each expands its scope, and it will not be long before whole industries are fully automated, from drawing board to finished product. This is being reflected in the bringing together of the acronyms to form the composite CAD/CAM. Nor is CAD/CAM limited to large industries. It is already a boon to many small industries and would be to many more if their managers could investigate its possibilities.

On-line and Real-time Processing

In the early days of computing, programming and operating computers were related tasks and programmers had to operate the computer to run their programs. With the introduction of operating systems and higher level computer languages, this was superseded by **batch processing** in which all programs and their data were sent to computer centres to be run. Operators were distinct from programmers and their duty was to load the programs (usually via the medium of punched cards, punched paper tape or magnetic tape) into the computer and receive the output (usually from a line printer) and return it to the programmer. Batch processing also included the running of large corporate jobs such as the weekly or monthly payroll, which in many organizations are still handled in this way.

In the early 1970s, advances in disk technology provided rapidly accessible secondary storage at a reasonable price. This, together with the development of work stations consisting of a keyboard and visual display unit (VDU) connected directly to the computer, introduced **on-line** working. In this, users input their commands directly to the computer and the machine's response is output on the VDU or on a printer. This mode of working was first used by programmers in the development of their programs. Instead of waiting overnight for batch processing, only to find that a small error had caused a failure, they could run their programs on-line, receive immediate results, and act accordingly.

With the development of the **database management system** (DBMS), which provided users with the ability to update and access data in the database by using simple commands, on-line working expanded in the scope of its applications. When micros arrived on the scene it was well established and was immediately the normal method of communicating with the microcomputer. A machine which can only support one terminal makes its full processing power available for the tasks arriving via that terminal. One which supports a number of terminals **time-shares** its resources between them.

A particular aspect of on-line working is **real-time** processing. This is necessary when it is important for inputs to the computer to be processed immediately, or within a very short time. Processors or computers being used for control often fall into this category. Examples are the control of the cycle of a washing machine, the fuel injection in a motor vehicle, the working environment of an aeroplane, or control of an industrial process. In these cases, inputs consist of monitored data such as temperature, pressure and variation in direction; processing consists of assessing these against stored values; and outputs consist of control signals which adjust the appropriate parameters. The input data must be processed so as to produce an output which will have an effect in 'real time'.

In both real-time and on-line processing, the computer may be removed by almost any distance from the workstation or controlled device. Communication between them may be via a direct connection, a network, either public or private, or, as in the case of a space vehicle, signals at radio frequencies. In any of these cases communication of data to and from the computer or processor is important.

CHAPTER 3
NETWORKS

As will be seen in Part II, data is stored in a computer in digital form. Fast communication between computers therefore depends on digital transmission and the information technology boom has only been possible because of the development of digital communications.

The move towards fully digital networks has had to take consideration of the existing analogue **public switched telephone networks** (PSTNs) which, throughout the world, are the dominant means of communication. These only arrived in 1875 with the invention of the telephone and it is ironic to note that line communication originated as a means of digital transmission when, in 1844, the first Morse Code telegraph link was established.

The telephone network took line communication into the homes of individuals and quickly overtook the telegraph network, which provided links only between centralized points. Later, a switched data communication service (telex) was introduced to customers' premises, but this did not result in a threat to the pre-eminence of telephony.

For many years the telephone and telex networks adequately met the world's communication needs by providing circuit switching for voice on the one hand and textual messages on the other. Then, in the 1960s, time-shared accessing of computers from remote terminals placed new demands on transmission. The most significant was that, since computers only generate digital signals, these had to be converted into an analogue form to make their transmission over the PSTN possible. This conversion was achieved by the **modem** (**mod**ulator/**dem**odulator).

The characteristics of an analogue PSTN, however, imposed restrictions on the use of modems. Transmission speeds were limited and network noise, acceptable to speech, caused relatively high error rates in data. The growth of data traffic in the late 1960s thus showed the need for a faster and more secure means of data communication. At the same time, the increasing need of computer systems to exchange data, not only within a country but internationally, led telecommunications administrations to start planning dedicated data networks. In some countries circuit switched data networks (networks in which a circuit, once provided by switching, remains dedicated to the call for its full duration) were introduced and this would have been the result globally had not packet switching entered the arena.

PACKET SWITCHING

The principle involved in packet switching is that data messages are divided into modules and slotted into **packets** for transmission. A message may therefore consist of a number of packets. Each of these is composed of binary bits and is of a fixed size and format. Each packet (see Figure 3.1) contains:

- the address of its destination,
- the address of its origin, which allows a request for retransmission to be dispatched if the packet becomes corrupted or fails to reach its destination,
- the packet sequence number, which allows reconstitution of the complete message,
- the data itself,
- an error check field.

When a packet has been assembled, it is transmitted by its originating **node** (switching unit or exchange) towards some

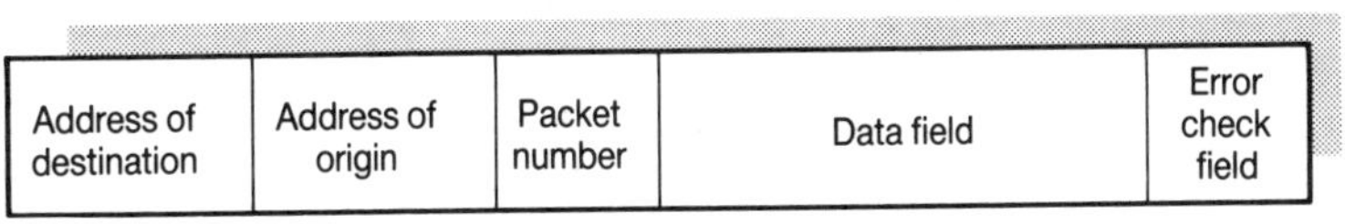

Figure 3.1 *Format of a typical packet.*

other node in the packet switched network. When it arrives there it undergoes an error check and is then retransmitted into the network. Each node transmits according to a routing algorithm based on the required destination and the availability of circuits. When a packet reaches its ultimate destination it is again checked for errors and the data extracted and stored in accordance with the packet number, so as to reconstitute the original message.

Packets may arrive out of sequence because of their different routings through the network. The receiving computer must then order them according to their sequence numbers. However, if an expected packet does not arrive within a given time, or if a packet arrives with an error, a request for retransmission is sent to the originating node.

The main functions of a packet switching system are storage and processing. These are typical computing functions and the exchanges in a packet switched network (network nodes) are therefore essentially computers. Thus, the network which is provided for communication between computers is operated by computers.

The advantage of packet switching is economy of line plant. In circuit switching, when a connection has been made between two points, the circuit is maintained for the duration of the communication. In packet switching, dedicated circuits are not established for messages, and packets to the same destination may be routed in various ways through the network, depending on circuit availability and loading. This results in packets for many destinations and comprising many messages sharing a common carrier.

Packet switching first became operational in private networks in the USA, but it was not long before public packet switched networks were installed in many countries. Now there are international connections between both public and private packet switched networks, allowing data to be made available to worldwide users. Thus universities, research establishments, banks and businesses are able to gain access to the data banks of collaborators, partners, subsidiaries, etc. Access can be restricted to those with the correct pass codes. This in turn allows commercial use to be made of the technology. Databases, such as for credit card checking, can be put at the disposal of those who pay for their use. This is an example of value added services, which are discussed below.

Local Area Networks (LANs)

LANs were developed to allow local computers to communicate with a central computer or with each other. They facilitate distributed processing and allow users to be serviced locally by small, cheap computers which store the data most necessary for local use and which access the data held on similar machines, or a central computer, via the LAN. Typically their nodes are less than 5 Km apart, often being within a single site or building, and are usually owned by a single organization.

Data is transmitted on LANs in the form of packets – though switching is not employed. High rates of transmission (10–100 Mbits/sec) are achieved and many LANs employ optical fibres as their transmission media. All the computers connected to a LAN need to prepare the data they want to transmit in the precise packet format which conforms to the LAN's protocols – otherwise the receiving computer would be unable to interpret it. Each computer must also have the software which dissembles the received packets and reconstructs the full messages. These processes are necessary overheads on each node of the LAN.

The configuration of a LAN takes the form of one of three basic architectures. The first is the 'shared bus' (see Figure 3.2), in which the computers usually take turns to send any packets which they wish to transmit – though in some networks the nodes dispatch packets as and when they need to. The popular Ethernet is an example of this type.

In the 'ring' architecture (see Figure 3.3), as in the shared bus, packets are dispatched onto a common highway for all nodes to examine their addresses, with only the destination node claiming the packet and extracting its data. The Cambridge Ring is an example.

The third fundamental LAN structure, the 'star' (see Figure 3.4), is most often employed when a number of computers of more or less equal status are all dependent on a central, more powerful facility, and are connected to it by dedicated links. Usually the central computer polls the others

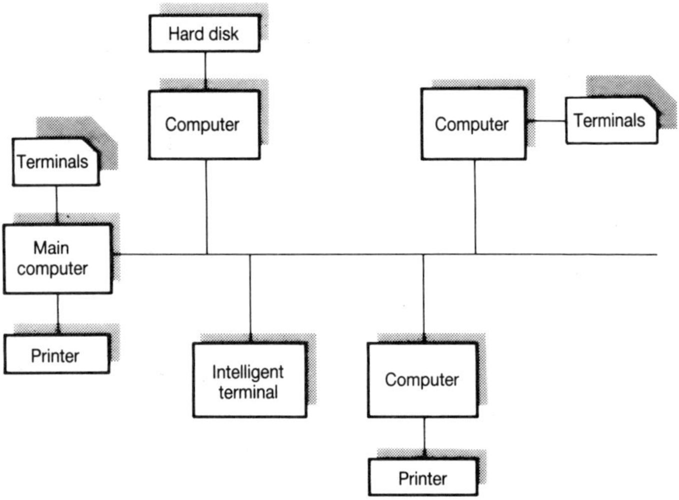

Figure 3.2 *Shared bus structured LAN.*

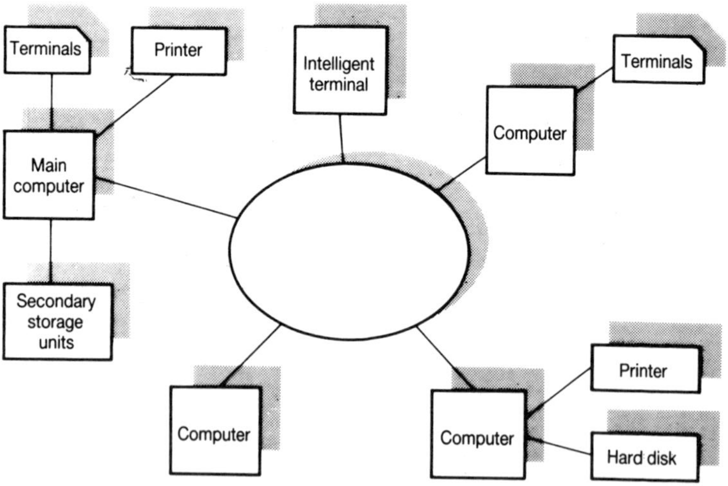

Figure 3.3 *Ring structured LAN.*

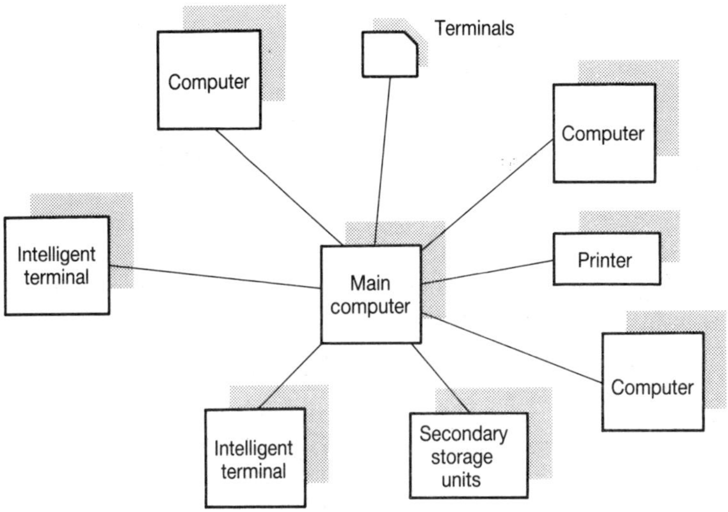

Figure 3.4 *Star structured LAN.*

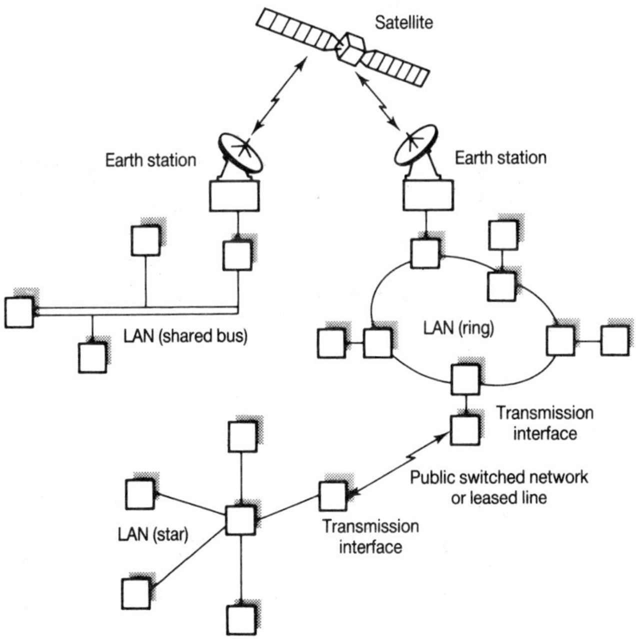

Figure 3.5 *Interconnected LANs.*

in turn, allowing them to transmit if they need to. It also acts as a switching node to allow communication between any two peripheral computers. A system in which a number of terminals, or micros, communicate with each other via a minicomputer (electronic mail) is an example of a star architecture.

Figure 3.5 shows each of these architectures and also how LANs may be interconnected to form a **wide area network** (WAN). This may be achieved using dedicated private circuits or via the PSTN. And either of these may, in turn, make use of cable or satellite connections.

A LAN may consist of a number of computers each of which generates a lot of information. There may be a main computer or all the nodes may be of equal status. On the other hand, a LAN may be such that a number of micros are provided with access to a larger machine which stores common data, provides storage for data generated by the nodes, and forms a switching point for communication between the nodes. In the modern office environment, it is often the case that a main central computer provides facilities, such as electronic mail and information services, to the managers' terminals.

Problems in Networking

Although LANs are now in common use, the setting up of a network between computers is not a trivial matter. It amounts to considerably more than simply plugging items of equipment together. This is due, mainly, to two reasons, cost and the lack of compatibility between different makes of equipment.

The problem of cost takes the form of hidden charges in the installation of a LAN. The cost of equipment, or the initial cost, may be discovered from the dealer – but, as well as computers, this needs to include printers, modems (if necessary), network interfaces and, above all, workstations and cable. The integrated cost may contain charges which had not been expected, at least in size. These include software development, software modification, staff training and maintenance. The labour involved in the installation of wiring can also amount to a substantial proportion. Running costs, such as the rental charges of communications links, should also be taken into account. It is therefore worth being sure of where workstations will be and how much wiring will be involved so that estimates for these costs can be made early.

The second major issue for consideration in planning interconnection is compatibility. It was mentioned above that the computers connected to a LAN all need to have the software necessary for sending and receiving packets in accordance with the **protocols** of that LAN. Different LANs have different protocols and, as yet, there is no agreed international standard to which adherence can be expected – although a number of standards have been proposed by various bodies, and these may be employed in certain LANs.

Starting with nothing, a user may overcome this difficulty by purchasing a single supplier's equipment. Even then, however, he may experience the problem when expansion becomes necessary. The original equipment may be obsolescent and the manufacturer's new range (if there is one) may not be an ideal choice – other than for reasons of compatibility. The manufacturer may have ceased trading. The technology leader in the field, perhaps an otherwise obvious choice, may not be compatible with the existing equipment.

Possible solutions are to introduce enough capacity at the outset to allow for foreseeable expansion, or to accept that the current system will be replaced entirely when expansion becomes necessary or when obsolescence sets in. Neither of these, however, overcome the problem of incompatibility between existing LANs or computers which need to be linked.

Recognized incompatibility is therefore a consideration in choosing equipment for interconnection. Apparent or partial compatibility can be an even greater problem. Many types of equipment have hardware compatibility, in that they are 'plug compatible', but they lack the full complement of software to handle the data that needs to be interchanged. This is clearly something to be checked before purchase.

INTEGRATED SERVICES DIGITAL NETWORK (ISDN)

In spite of the increase in data traffic and the proliferation of packet switched networks, telephone traffic is still the dominant force in world communications and PSTNs still infuence how transmission is achieved. However, advancing technology is influencing the world's PSTNs. The new generation of telephone exchanges is based on computer control and digital switching; signalling between exchanges is derived from packet formatted interprocessor communication; transmission is also digital, in the form of pulse code modulation, in which messages are coded into binary bits which are sent at a rate of 2.048 Mbits/sec. PSTNs all over the world are thus becoming digital. They are transmitting voice traffic in digital form and are consequently able, without any need of conversion, to carry directly-input computer data.

While the technology has advanced to allow the integration of voice and data transmission, the number of communications services being offered to the public is increasing. To avoid the cost of a separate network for each service (telephony, data, telex, facsimile, etc.) there is a need for an integrated services network. Indeed, plans exist for ISDNs which have common inputs for voice and data traffic, the distinction being made only by customers' terminal equipment.

ISDNs will offer a circuit switched data network alongside the now well established interconnection of packet switched networks. The indications are that there is room for both and, indeed, that they will be interconnected.

VALUE ADDED NETWORKS (VANS)

It is expected that ISDNs will not only be carriers of telephone traffic and computer data, but providers of services such as facsimile, telex, access to databases or processing facilities, dispatch of messages to a number of simultaneous destinations selected from a bank of addresses stored in the system by the sender (electronic mail), and many others.

Meanwhile many such services are provided as **value added networks** (VANs). A VAN is created when a provider offers a service via the telephone network, so that it 'adds value' to the telephone connection above and beyond its ability to carry voice or data traffic. In this context a VAN implies the use of a computer to provide the service.

Examples of existing VANs are the provision of processing facilities, access to information libraries, facsimile, electronic transfer of funds, electronic mail and credit card processing. The principle involved is that users of the service gain access by inserting one or more pass codes which allow entry into the system, or selected parts of it. Defined commands or queries then extract the information or activate the service required. Each access is monitored and charged for.

VANs are as yet in their infancy, but it will not be long before the services provided by electronic communications are numerous. Indeed the bond of marriage between computers and communications is already so secure that some of these services are even now being taken for granted.

CHAPTER 4

OVERVIEW OF A COMPUTER SYSTEM DEVELOPMENT PROJECT

It is now quite commonplace for a manager to have to decide whether a task should be computerized. Technical managers are taking advantage of modern technology to automate engineering processes; office functions are being computerized in departments of all sizes; small businesses are using computers for accounting, inventory control, customer lists and many other purposes. In general, users of information of all types are realizing that computers can make their jobs easier.

Choosing and developing computer systems are not, however, trivial tasks. It is true that home computer enthusiasts can write programs quite quickly, and this often gives them the impression that all programming is easy. Such people, who do not realize how much knowledge they lack, can be very persuasive when advising a manager that they could provide and program a computer system for less than half of what a contractor would charge.

However, there is more to a computer system than rapid programming. A thorough study needs to be carried out to ensure that the correct hardware is purchased. The software that is written needs to be maintainable: it must be well designed, well structured and well documented. At some time in the future – usually as soon as the system is in service – it will need to be corrected, expanded or modified for some other reason. It must also be thoroughly tested before being brought into service, if it is to be reliable. A business has more stringent requirements than a home user and cannot afford the losses of time or data which may result from an unprofessionally developed system.

With the proliferation of microcomputers, peripherals and software packages on the market, it is often possible for the requirements for a small system to be fulfilled 'off the shelf'. Advice on purchasing a micro system is therefore offered in the next chapter. Beyond that, it is recommended that if a computer larger than a micro is necessary, or if the required software is not available in proprietary form and applications programming is necessary, assistance be sought from computer professionals.

This advice cannot be emphasized too strongly. It is not uncommon for amateurs to develop, or partially develop, a system and then not be able to find the faults in it. The time and money lost when this occurs in the development phase of a project can be significant. When it happens after the system has been put into service, it can be catastrophic, particularly if adequate security procedures have not been introduced to safeguard the company's files or services.

For those managers who may need to put the development of a computer system out to contract, this chapter offers an insight into the progress of such a project and the manager's responsibilities in it.

SYSTEM LIFE CYCLE

The life cycle of a computer system is illustrated in Figure 4.1. Like that of any other system, it commences with the ideas that conceive it, progresses through the development and operational stages and ends with the closure and recovery of the system.

The initial ideas invariably concern the purpose of the system rather than its type. The users are concerned with what they want the system to do, and this is how it should be. Too often, however, in specifying their requirements, the users try to design the system instead of defining its functional and environmental requirements.

In most businesses, a formal project is not initiated until it has been shown to be economically viable and this usually means that a feasibility study must be conducted. Once the project has been shown to 'cost in' and authority has been given for its commencement, a full **specification of requirements** (SOR) of the system needs to be prepared.

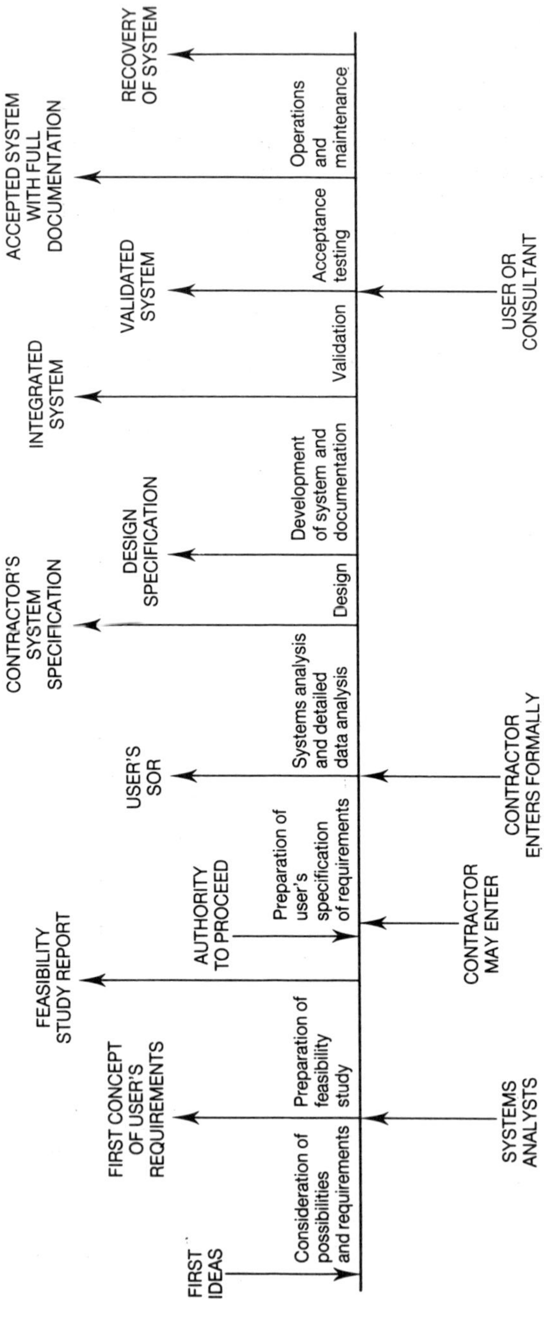

Figure 4.1 *Life cycle of a computer system.*

REQUIREMENTS OF THE SYSTEM

The first point to be made is that the SOR is the user's responsibility. The user must prepare it and verify it. Any error may be taken by the contractor as a basis for design and become a part of the resulting computer system. In the worst case, an error in the SOR could result in inappropriate hardware being purchased and incorrect and/or unnecessary software being developed. This is expensive to rectify. Indeed, the cost of correcting errors during the system's life cycle approximately follows the 'factor of ten' rule. This states that an error which would require one unit of cost for its repair if found at the specification stage costs ten units at the design stage, 100 at the code stage and 1000 at the operational stage (see Figure 4.2).

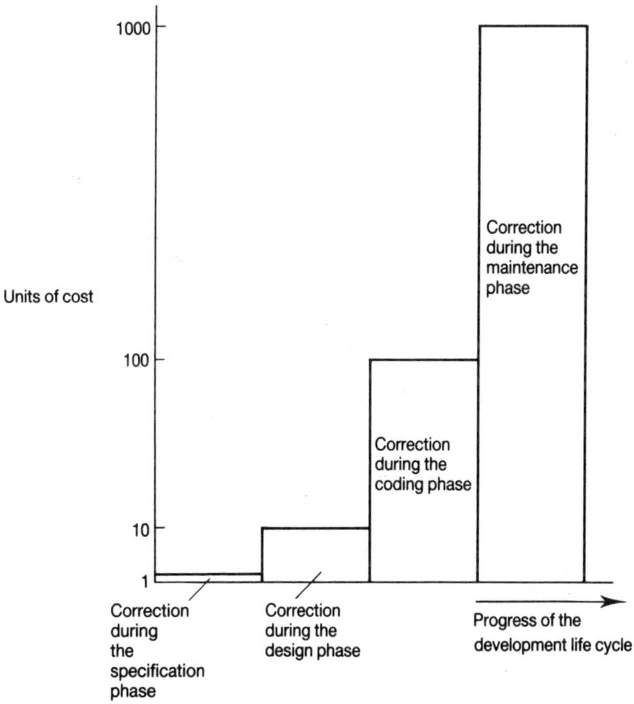

Figure 4.2 *'Factor of ten' rule for the cost of correcting specification errors.*

It is thus important for the SOR to be both complete and correct. Yet, for a number of reasons, it is the most difficult stage of a project in which to achieve either completeness or correctness. It is also the stage to which formal verification methods are least applied.

In many organizations, SORs are poor, not only due to real difficulties, but also because they are treated casually. They are often thought of as something to be got out of the way as quickly as possible so that the 'real work' can begin. Inadequate knowledge, poor style and culpable attitudes lead to poor SORs. Most computer projects go wrong at some time, and many do so because of inadequacies in the SOR. An inadequate, badly written or incorrect SOR leads to projects in some cases being aborted and, in others, corrected. In all cases time and money are wasted.

A computer system may be required to perform tasks which have previously been carried out (1) not at all, (2) manually, semi-automatically or electromechanically, or (3) by another computer. In the first case, there is no precedent for the requirements of the new system. New facilities are added to the developing specification as ideas arise, and changes are frequent.

In the second case a precedent exists, but improved facilities are demanded. New ways of working, so as to derive greatest benefit from computerization, may be necessary and, if they are not recognized at first, they are introduced later after experience of the computer system has been gained. Recognition of optimum ways of working is often an evolutionary process rather than a spontaneous one, and this necessitates changes even after the system is in service.

In the third case there is a precedent, and perhaps even an earlier SOR, but, almost invariably, substantial changes are required. Improved facilities, greater reliability, new forms of output, and interaction with peripheral equipment of later technology are typical examples. Verification of the new SOR against the old one can therefore at best be partial; it is often misleading.

In all cases the requirements for the new system evolve. There is at all times the possibility of new ideas or the recognition of better methods or facilities. Indeed, when the system is installed and the user has become familiar with it, there is usually a spate of requests for changes, and this leads to expensive and often difficult modification of the system.

There is therefore a genuine problem for the user in knowing what to specify in the SOR. There are times when he thinks he knows, but inevitably there will be changes. In order, therefore, that the SOR may be as thorough as possible, it should be the result of an extensive systems analysis. Only then can there be a reasonable chance of completeness and correctness.

Systems analysis involves the study and documentation of all aspects of the requirements of the proposed system. Its purpose is to achieve a full and accurate SOR. The ultimate definition of the appropriate hardware and software depends on such factors as how much data the processor has to handle, the manner of arrival of the data (e.g. on tape or floppy disk, or over a data communications link), how much data must be stored at a time, the types of output required, how many terminals need to be supported, whether there is interaction with other computers, the system software necessary, and the environment in which the computer must operate. Until these and other questions are answered in detail, a system to meet the requirements cannot be developed or purchased.

The information necessary for preparing the SOR is typically held by the user. However, since he may not be aware of how to document it, or even what information is required, the use of a systems analyst is usually a good investment. The analyst must extract from the user the information required and document it in a form suitable for a contractor's acceptance: he must bridge the gap between the user and the contractor. To do this, he must possess certain skills:

- he must be analytical and have a disciplined approach and orderly mind;
- he must have very good communication skills, both oral and written and a good interviewing technique;
- he must be trained in what information to seek, where to look for it and how to relate it to the overall picture once he has found it.

Systems analysis is not a trivial task, but it is often trivialized and executed badly by ex-programmers who are untrained and unsuited to the task. In the interest of maximizing the completeness and correctness of the SOR, it is often worthwhile for a user to employ a reputable consultant to carry out the systems analysis.

In the end, however, while it is essential to produce as good an SOR as possible, it is necessary to recognize that the user is unlikely to succeed in producing a perfect and unchanging SOR. To allow for the expected changes, it is best to initiate a formal process of change control between the user and the contractor. The process is shown in Figure 4.3, which also shows an onus on the contractor to design for flexibility in anticipation of further changes to the requirements.

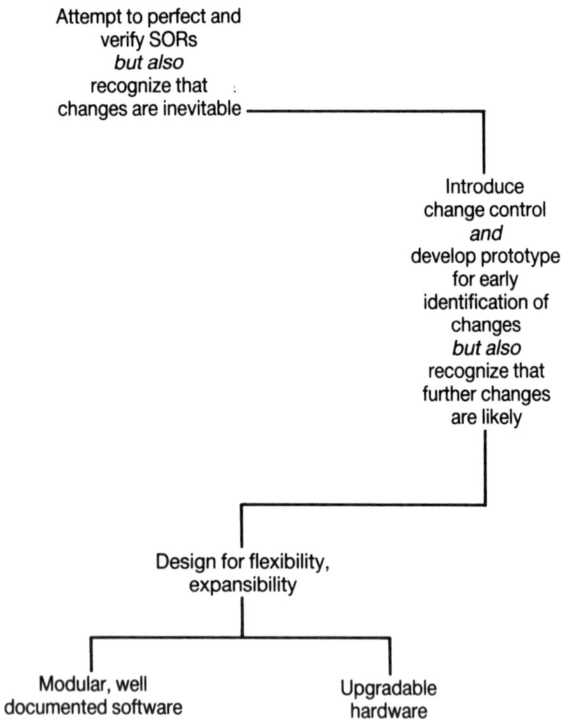

Figure 4.3 *Minimizing the problems of specification.*

PROTOTYPING

The high likelihood of the user changing or adding to the SOR during development, or indeed after the system is operational, has already been remarked on. And this likelihood will not be eliminated entirely by improving the quality of SORs. The fact is that until the user has experience of a system he cannot envisage many of the facilities which it could offer. It has been estimated that, on average, 60–70% of the software effort invested in a system is during the maintenance phase, i.e. after the system is in service, and most of this effort is in adaptive or perfective rather than corrective maintenance. The way to reduce this maintenance effort is to provide the user with experience of the system during the development phase. If this is not to delay bringing the system into service, it implies **prototyping.**

Prototyping allows the gaps, or probable gaps, in the SOR to be filled in a methodical and efficient manner prior to acceptance testing. It improves the chance of achieving a satisfactory end product in spite of the likely inadequacies of the initial SOR and it allows modifications, which would otherwise have occurred in the maintenance phase, to be identified and implemented in the development phase.

The first kind of prototype is a simulation, usually quite simply contrived, of the system or certain aspects of it. This is useful for showing the user what computer output formats are expected to look like so that he can get an early idea of how the contractor has interpreted his requirements. This kind of prototype is also useful for operators. They can be given an early preview of the aspects of the system which they will have to work with, so that ergonomic and other problems can be corrected prior to development. Almost invariably, changes are requested.

The second type of prototype is the system model, intended to exhibit the attributes of the final system operationally, functionally, or both. On this, computer operators and terminal users can perform their functions as they would eventually do on the developed system. Appropriate modifications can thus be requested, implemented and reviewed. There are two sub-sets of this kind of prototype. One is a 'throwaway' model whose life ends when its purpose as a prototype is accomplished. The other will evolve into the final system. The latter is useful when the final system is one-off, since the cost of the prototype goes directly towards building the final system; the throwaway prototype is more acceptable, and its cost more easily accommodated in the total costs, when the final system is to be replicated.

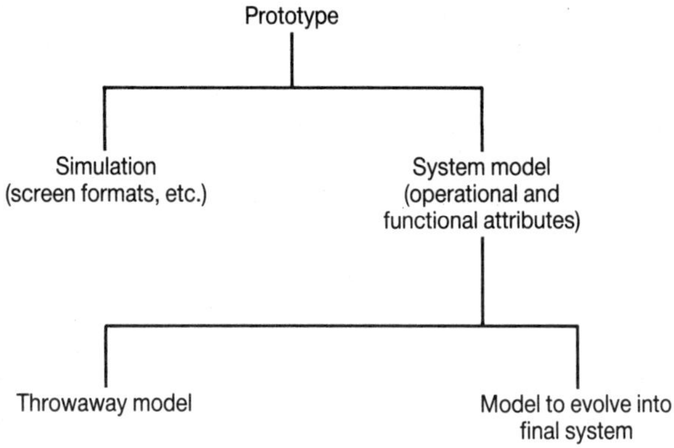

Figure 4.4 *Prototyping.*

Figure 4.4 illustrates the aspects of prototyping. Whichever type is employed, the principle of providing the user with early experience of the proposed system, modifying the prototype in accordance with his requests, reviewing these and iterating towards an ideal system, is one which goes a long way to mitigating the problems inherent in SOR production.

VERIFICATION AND VALIDATION

It is seen from Figure 4.1 that a project consists of a number of phases of activity, separated by points at which these activities terminate in the production of some proof of their success. These proofs take the form of documents or completed modules of the system itself.

Each stage is in fact a translation of its predecessor into a form which is one step closer to the final product. In interpreting one stage into the next, no attention is normally paid to earlier stages. Indeed, each translation requires different expertise and so translators (who are the workers on the various aspects of the project) may not be competent to seek information from earlier stages. For example, a programmer writes programs to meet the designer's specification, and is unlikely either to have the opportunity or the competence to check whether the design is a faithful translation of the user's SOR. It is therefore essential to the success of the project that any one stage is correct before it is used as the basis of translation into the next stage. If it were not, the error would be compounded as it rippled down through the stages and would probably not be discovered until the **target system** was tested. By then the effort and cost required to correct it could be considerable (see Figure 4.2).

The process of testing each stage of a project, by comparing it with its predecessor, to determine whether there is a faithful translation, is known as **verification**. The methods of verification depend on the stage being tested and the type of system being developed, and a great many have been devised. These range from simple **peer checks** of programs and documents to elaborate mathematical proofs of correctness.

If an error in the production of one stage goes undetected, it will become an accepted aspect of that phase and will comprise the criteria against which the succeeding stage will be verified. Later verification will therefore not discover it and it will only come to light when the developed system is tested against the requirements laid down in the original user's SOR. This testing against original requirements, under operational conditions, is known as **validation**.

The tests for validation will depend on the functions of the system, but they should always be designed when the SOR has been verified and not at the time of validation. Their purpose is to test functionality and they should therefore not be influenced by the design of the system. Indeed, it is suggested that an independent team should design both the verification and validation tests and analyse their results. This certainly maximizes the integrity of the tests and the interpretation of their results, but it is all too infrequently observed.

Verification and validation testing during system development are the responsibilities of the contractor. The user, however, is responsible for acceptance testing, which is discussed below. As a final comment, it should be noted that verification and validation testing are intended to discover errors, not to prove that there are no errors. In general, it is not possible to prove conclusively that there are no errors in software – only that none has been exposed by given tests or during operation. It is possible to give the impression of superior software by testing it inadequately or with poorly designed tests.

DEVELOPMENT

Computer system development is normally carried out in a sequence of well defined stages. Figure 4.5 shows a simplified view of the procedure.

When the SOR has been verified, the contractor must propose a computer system to meet the stated requirements. This is achieved by analysts who need to be familiar with the tasks demanded of the computer system. In a business environment, **systems analysts** are generally employed for this. For technical applications, knowledge specific to the application, as well as computer system expertise, is necessary.

In all cases, a large part of the job is data analysis. A computer is basically an information handler and, whatever its environment, its task is ultimately to receive information, process it and output results. The power of the computer required, the size of its store, and the types, quality and quantity of peripheral equipment will all depend on the amount of data to be handled, the rate of its arrival, the volume to be stored, the amount of processing on each item of data, and the required response time. The type of computer is further defined by the number of simultaneous inputs it must handle, the system software and the structure of applications software most appropriate to the application. Data analysis of the system is therefore of extreme importance and it is only by carrying out this task thoroughly that a computer system can be specified with confidence to satisfy the SOR.

A great deal more work will have gone into preparing the **system specification** (a specification of the system being proposed to meet the SOR) than went into a proposal which might have been put forward in a feasibility study. The user is now able to compare the actual cost of the recommended system with the authorized budget for the project. He is also in

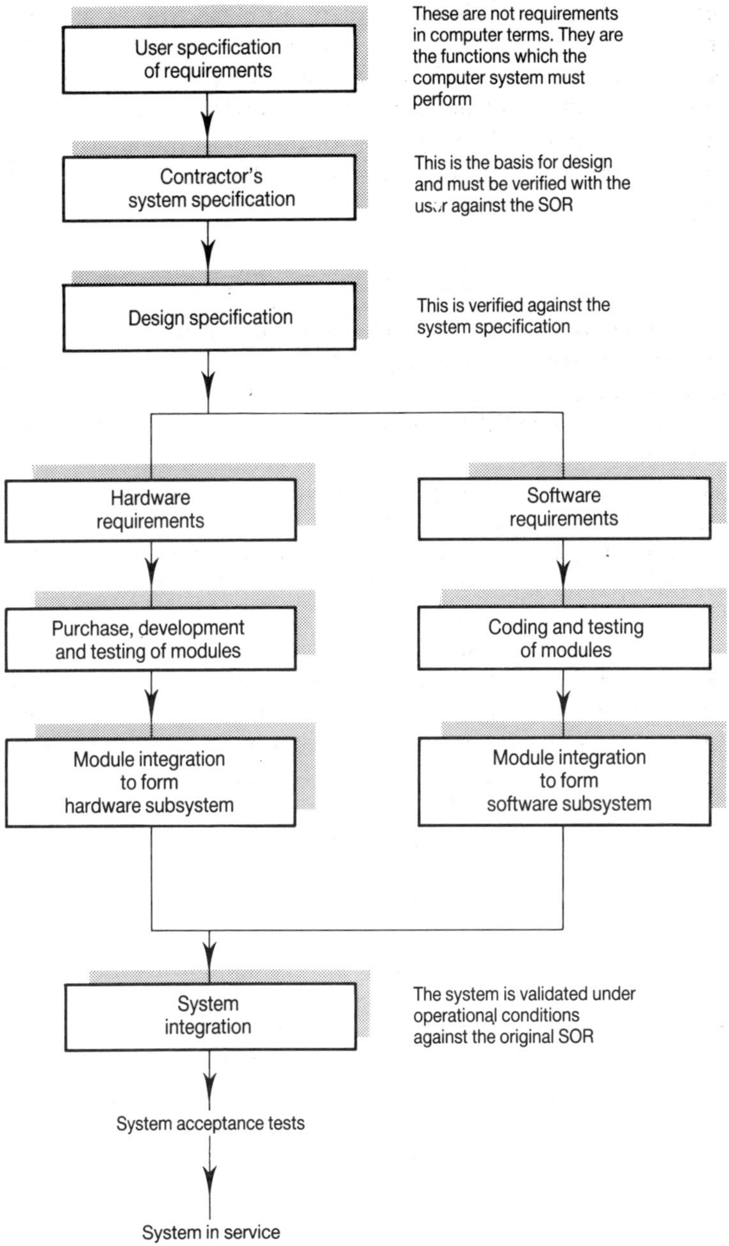

Figure 4.5 *Outline of the development of a computer system.*

possession of more accurate estimates of project timescales. He should verify the system specification by checking that the functions which the contractor's analysts have defined for the system are those which he intended to specify in the SOR.

With the system specification verified, the computer system and its functions defined, and the data categorized, the designers can commence their work. The hardware and system software are purchased, tested as individual items, integrated and verified as a subsystem. The applications software is defined as functions, then as smaller and smaller units. Databases are defined from the data relationships discoverd and defined during the data analysis. Then coding takes place, with each software module being tested individually. Test data is designed to check outputs for all possible inputs, both valid and invalid – so that modules are tested for completeness as well as correctness. Then the integration of modules is carried out, with integration testing being performed at every step until, ultimately, the whole software subsystem has been integrated and verified.

Finally, the hardware and software subsystems are integrated and, when the full system has been verified under test conditions, it is validated under operational conditions against the user's original requirements. If the system has passed its validation tests, the contractor is confident of its ability to carry out the functions demanded of it in the SOR. The system is then ready for acceptance testing, on-site, according to a test schedule agreed between the user and the contractor. The user is in fact responsible for defining the acceptance tests and for overseeing them. In practice, it is often sensible for user and contractor to prepare them jointly. This provides a further opportunity to verify the contractor's understanding of the SOR. It also minimizes the probability of disagreement, at the time of acceptance testing, as to whether the tests are valid. Clearly, criteria for passing the tests should also be agreed in advance.

MAINTENANCE

Any work carried out on the system after its installation and acceptance is considered to be maintenance. This can be:

- **corrective**, which is in response to actual errors;
- **adaptive**, which introduces modifications essential for the system to continue functioning effectively in a changed environment; or
- **perfective**, which introduces changes not essential to effective working but which may improve efficiency, or maintainability.

It has been estimated that, on average, 60–70% of the total software effort on a system is expended as maintenance. It is therefore important that the system is maintainable, and maintainability is achieved at the design stage by using high level languages, modern design and programming methods, and producing good documentation at all stages of the development. Design and development should therefore be carried out with maintenance in mind, and this is the responsibility of the contractor. However, it carries an implicit warning to the user. He needs to state the criteria for acceptance of the system in the SOR and these criteria should include documentation of a defined quality. Indeed, the quality assurance methods employed by the contractor throughout the project should be examined and approved before the contract is placed.

Any maintenance effort is likely to change the system and thus affect maintainability. Often the user's staff are involved in this but, whoever the maintainers are, they need to inherit a maintainable system from the contractors in order to carry out their tasks efficiently. They then need to keep the system maintainable in order that later maintainers can also carry out their tasks. Maintenance should therefore be carried out with maintenance in mind – for example, by testing all changed software thoroughly and by keeping all documentation up-to-date.

Responsibilities of User and Contractor

Finally, it may be useful to summarize the main responsibilities of user and contractor through the development of a computer system.

User To provide a complete, correct and unambiguous SOR. This implies assigning a systems analyst to study the requirements and write the document. Standards of form and content should be adhered to in its production; individual users should devote time to defining their requirements and verifying them by reviewing the completed SOR; the analyst should consider operational and environmental as well as functional matters; and the SOR should be a statement of requirements and not an attempt at system design. It should also state what documentation must be provided with the system, and its quality. Indeed, it is also necessary to agree with the contractor what methods of quality assurance will be applied throughout the project.

Contractor To study the SOR and seek clarification of any uncertainties or ambiguities. Further, the contractor should be encouraged to question the need for specified facilities if they appear to be illogical or unnecessary.

Contractor To interpret the SOR into a system specification and to present this to the user for discussion and verification.

User To study the system specification carefully, compare it with the SOR for completeness and correctness and, in understanding it as the contractor's interpretation of the SOR, to use it as a means of verifying the SOR.

User and Contractor To adjust the SOR and system specification until users' requirements are clear and well documented and their interpretation into the system specification is understood and agreed.

User and Contractor To agree a change control procedure so that new and changed requirements meet with a formal method of presentation, documentation, review and implementation. This ensures that they are handled optimally and that the contractor receives credit for extra work rather than disparagement for delays to the project.

Contractor To recognize that the user will only appreciate the possibilities of the system after he is familiar with it and, if at all possible, to provide a prototype at an early stage of development.

User To use the prototype and become familiar with it.

User and Contractor To explore changes to the prototype so as to iterate towards an optimal system.

Contractor To recognize that later changes are inevitable and to cater for these by designing for flexibility and expandability.

User To design system acceptance tests, based on functionality as stated in the SOR, and agree them, the method of applying them, and the criteria for the system's acceptance with the contractor. It may be necessary to employ consultants to assist with this.

Contractor To study the proposed acceptance tests and compare them with the SOR. This is another opportunity to verify the SOR, for the user may be setting out to test a function which he thinks he has specified but which the contractor has not understood to be in the SOR.

Contractor To employ good verification at every stage of the development so as to ensure that the SOR and later legitimate changes are translated faithfully into an effective final product. Also to validate the operational system against the SOR and the later changes.

CHAPTER 5

BUYING A MICROCOMPUTER

Until a few years ago, a firm with a computer installation almost certainly employed professional computer staff to manage it. More recently, low priced and easy-to-handle microcomputers have brought computing into the office environment and it is now commonplace for micros to be bought and put to use without the assistance of computer professionals. However, although microcomputers are cheap, a useful system is more expensive than advertising may imply. When the costs of software, installation, maintenance contracts and peripherals such as terminals and printers are added, the computer itself accounts for only about twenty per cent of the total installed system cost. The choice of equipment is therefore important.

Moreover, the greater the reliance placed on the computer system, once it has been acquired, the greater the penalty for its failure. The system must, therefore, be properly operated and maintained. Indeed, firms have gone out of business because their accounts, customer lists, inventory records or payrolls have been entrusted to a computer and then lost due to incorrect operation and lack of security copies of the files.

This chapter offers advice on the selection of a computer system. The advice is necessarily general and is in the nature of a way of thinking and what questions to ask. It cannot be considered complete, as each situation makes its own unique demands. An assumption must be that a prospective computer system purchaser has a good appreciation of the purpose for which it is required. This chapter, however, does not assume computer literacy on the part of the reader, though an appreciation of the fundamentals of computers – as can be acquired from Part II – would be of great value in choosing a system.

It must also be emphasized that this chapter is concerned only with micros. The purchase of mainframes or minis is a matter for high level management decision, with professional advice. Further, as emphasized in the previous chapter, the development of any computer system for which applications programming must be carried out also demands professional advice. In addition, although this chapter addresses business users in particular, the advice given applies to all prospective computer system purchasers.

CONSULTANTS AND DEALERS

It is first important to know exactly what the computer is required for – what is to be computerized and what tasks the computer will be required to perform. It is essential to be quite clear about this, for only then can the most appropriate computer system be selected with confidence. If the computer system is likely to be simple, the manager may choose to analyse the job and select a system himself, perhaps with the help of a dealer. If, however, it is not small, or if programming is involved, professional advice should be sought.

If there is no computer expertise within the firm to call on, it may be appropriate to employ an independent consultant. However, care is needed on three counts.

First, it should be ensured that he is a true professional – that he has been in the business for a considerable time and that he is a member of an appropriate professional body. An idea of his professionalism may be obtained by talking to some of his previous clients. If he refuses to refer to earlier clients, he probably does not have a history of success.

Second, it should be ensured that he is truly independent. Many so-called consultants have links with computer firms, and these are more likely to recommend systems in which they have an interest than those which best suit their clients' purposes.

Third, his charges need to be established before he is hired. Consultants usually charge by the day and, if efficient use is not made of their time, the penalty can be high.

As an approximate guide, it is usually cost effective to

engage a consultant if the cost of the project is above about £20 000. If the cost is below this, the purchaser may need to seek advice from a computer dealer and have recourse to his own knowledge. The remainder of this chapter is intended to provide advice for a purchaser in this situation.

The first thing for the purchaser to do is to prepare a written specification of requirements prior to seeking to purchase a computer system to fulfil them. This was shown in the previous chapter to be essential when going out to contract and, in buying a micro system off the shelf, it offers the same advantages. It helps to clarify thoughts and ideas and minimizes the chance of the purchaser being talked into making inappropriate or unnecessary purchases. Further, the finished document increases the chance of considering all factors which might have a bearing on the choice of system. It is also as well to give the dealer a copy. This will help him to understand the requirements, lead him to ask questions where clarification is needed, and offer the best chance of his giving good advice. Moreover, it has the added advantage of covering the purchaser, in the UK at least, against being sold a system which does not meet the requirements. In British law, under the Sale of Goods Act, 1893

> 'where the buyer, expressly or by implication, makes known to the seller the particular purpose for which the goods are required, so as to show that the buyer relies on the seller's skill or judgement, and the goods are of a description which it is in the course of the seller's business to supply (whether he be the manufacturer or not), there is an implied condition that the goods should be reasonably fit for such purpose . . .'

With computers being cheap and numerous, it is inevitable that standards among dealers vary. Many salesmen have very limited knowledge of computers, many are unscrupulous, and many have ties to certain manufacturers, which they do not readily reveal. Before accepting the advice of a dealer, or buying from him, it is worth establishing that he has no vested interests and that he does have a good knowledge of his subject. A few questions to which the purchaser already knows the answers should give a feel for how sound the dealer's knowledge base is, as will the level of his explanations. If he consistently speaks 'above your head' rather than at an understandable level, his knowledge, even if existent, is not being put at the purchaser's disposal.

Before a purchaser commits himself, he should expect an extensive demonstration of the system. It is therefore a good idea to test the dealer at an early stage on how well he understands and can demonstrate both his hardware and software.

The dealer's credibility is also revealed in what he offers in terms of warranty on equipment and maintenance contracts and what facilities or arrangements he can provide for training. Further, his line of talk should show that he is not just trying to sell a computer, but that he is attempting to understand the purchaser's problem so as to recommend the most appropriate computer to solve it. If a dealer does not prove satisfactory on all these matters, another should be sought – there are plenty around.

SOFTWARE AND SYSTEM CONSIDERATIONS

Selecting a computer consists of choosing a *system* and not just hardware. Indeed, the choice of hardware is strongly influenced by the software that must run on it. For example, there are now a number of software packages written to computerize specific areas of work in a number of professions – such as accounting, legal and medical. It would be gross folly for an accountant to purchase an excellent computer only to find it useless because the software which he needs was not written to run on it.

This may seem a silly mistake to make, and it is, but it happens all the time. There are so many matters to consider that any one criterion may be overlooked, especially when a dealer is proving how marvellous a certain computer is. A written and verified specification of requirements minimizes the chance of neglecting important criteria. A **decision matrix** (as in Table 5.1) provides both a visual summary of the major elements of the SOR and an aid to ensuring that all essential components are obtained – even when compromises have to be made.

Another major consideration is the operating system. If a computer is being purchased, along with pre-written software,

Table 5.1 *Decision matrix to assist in selecting the components of a computer system (lists are not exhaustive)*

Item	*Essential*	*Would be nice*	*Unnecessary*
Hardware			
Processor → single user			√
Processor – multi-user	√		
Spare processor		√	
Terminals	4	+2	
Floppy disk	√		
Hard disk	√		
Letter quality printer		√	
Fast printer	√		
Software			
Operating system	√		
DBMS			√
Accounts package		√	
Spreadsheet	√		
Word processor	√		
Spelling checker	√		
Compiler			√
Services			
Delivery	√		
Installation	√		
Maintenance contract	√		
Training			√

for a specific purpose, for example to perform certain fixed functions in a doctor's surgery, there may only be one software package available for the job. It would then be necessary to purchase this, along with the hardware and system software which will run it. In other words, the software packages required at the time of purchase may influence the choice of system. However, if a computer system is being purchased for more general purposes, it is advisable to acquire a widely used operating system. There will be more software written to run on this and the ability to take advantage of new software in the future will be enhanced.

Care is needed if a database management system (DBMS) is required. Although there are versions of DBMS designed for use on micros, they usually require a great deal of memory, including a hard disk, and the latter can add significantly to the total cost of the system. Further, accessing databases is a complex process within the machine, and response times can be lengthy – particularly when frequent access to disk storage is involved.

The size of the database and the DBMS used will have an influence on how much memory is needed and how powerful a processor is necessary to manage this memory. The response times expected from the computer will also determine the power of the processor. Staff find long response times frustrating and often prefer to return to a manual paper system than to suffer a long wait at a terminal for a computer to respond to their requests.

Writing software is another consideration. A user needs to know whether he wishes only to use purchased software packages or whether he needs also to write his own applications programs. This, as a general principle, has been advised against, but there are occasions on which systems are purchased expressly to allow programming. This must then have a bearing on the choice of system software. For instance, a suitable language must be chosen and a compiler for that language needs to be available on the selected system. Two languages very popular for general programming on micros are BASIC and Pascal. The former is a very simple language and is almost universally available on micros and, though compilers are now available, its use has traditionally been effected by means of interpreters. Pascal has the advantage of being a more structured language which encourages programmers to employ better design and programming standards. In addition there are now program generators designed to ease the task of programming, and information on these should be sought from the dealer. The trade and professional press is also a useful source of information on new products.

Hardware Considerations

There are many aspects of hardware which affect the choice of computer. As far as processor power is concerned, one option is to acquire a processor of much greater capacity than could possibly be needed. It is assumed, however, that cost is a significant criterion and, therefore, that overspending is undesirable. Some of the criteria having a bearing on power, such as acceptable database access and terminal user response times, have already been discussed.

A question which has a bearing on power, but which is also an issue in itself, is whether a single-user or a multi-user system is required. If the latter, then how many terminals does it need to sustain? It should be ensured that the computer has sufficient ports to accommodate not only the terminals required at the time of purchase, but also those expected in the future. Further, many systems offer a larger number of ports than they can serve concurrently while offering an acceptable response time to each. Published figures may have been calculated on the assumption that only a small percentage of the terminals will be in use at any time. Before purchase, it is necessary to determine the maximum number of terminals likely to operate concurrently so that a system can be chosen to provide not only the ports, but also the desired response times.

Once they are familiar with their systems, most computer users desire enhancements to be made. They want more terminal users, which require more ports and more power; and they want more facilities, which require more software and more memory. If this is likely to be the case, it is important to purchase a system which is expandable, in the sense that further memory, as well as more peripherals (disks, printers, etc.), can be added to it. A number of manufacturers make a range of computers rather than a single model. If the models in the range are **upward compatible** then, as a less powerful model is replaced by a more powerful one, with more facilities, all the software can be transferred without modification from one to the other. It is often not worth spending the extra money on the more powerful machine in the first place, but if there is a likelihood of a need to **upgrade** the processor, then it is as well to choose a machine which is part of an existing or planned range. This will incur a considerable saving, in that while processor power is increased, software and peripheral equipment do not need to be replaced.

In the realm of peripherals come printers, disk units and display terminals. There is a wide range of printers on the market and some are exceedingly slow. It is easy to be convinced that a given time to print a sheet of paper is 'really quite acceptable', but sitting and waiting for a twenty-page document to be printed soon reveals just how unacceptable it really is – particularly if each sheet of paper has to be input manually. If there will be much printing to be done, a fast, automatic-feed printer is a wise investment. Print quality too should be considered. For some uses, fast printers with somewhat inferior type are quite adequate; for others, only the most expensive **letter quality** printers would be acceptable.

Disk storage too is critical. Floppy and hard disks have different storage capacities and different access times and equipment should be chosen to be compatible with the requirements. If the system is to be used for the permanent storage of files, then data acquired, calculated and updated by the computer will need to be **dumped** to secondary storage for security at regular intervals, and at least each evening. It is as well to ensure that the procedures for this are simple (preferably automatic) and quick, or the risk of data loss will be increased, and carrying out the security dumps will take a great deal of time.

Diverse too are the options and prices of display terminals. There are many which appear beautifully compact and 'cute' but which offer a very inadequate display – except perhaps for text editing. The **resolution** too should be considered. If, for instance, it is important to have graphical displays, the best software graphics packages are wasted unless the display is of high resolution. Again, total requirements should be considered before deciding on display equipment.

Finally, it is necessary to ensure that all the chosen items of peripheral equipment will work with the selected processor. Often compromise choices must be made because the best individual equipment choices are incompatible. Even when compatibility is assured, it is sometimes the case that the dealer omits to mention that special software is required – and this of course increases the cost. It is well worth requesting a demonstration of the complete system on the dealer's premises before making a final decision. This has the further advantage of ensuring that the equipment and software being offered by the dealer actually exist. With new developments frequently appearing and competition being fierce, it is not unusual for hardware and software to be marketed before it is available. Many purchasers have acquired a system only to find that an essential component won't be available until 'next month'. Often they have not received it after a year.

It is also as well to determine whether any of the equipment, particularly the processor, needs a controlled environment in which to operate. This includes air conditioning and a special power supply. Operational figures, such as temperature ranges, should be requested, and vague terms like 'room temperature' should not be relied on. For example, equipment intended (and advertised) to function at room temperature in a temperate climate may not do so reliably in a tropical country, or in an environment with a high relative humidity.

Finally, the durability of the manufacturer should be considered. An opinion on whether a company will exist in a year's time is necessarily subjective but, with the rate of bankruptcies among computer firms being high, it is as well to have confidence in the chosen manufacturer's future. Maintenance, training and expansion of the system may depend on it.

OPERATION AND MAINTENANCE

Once a computer has been acquired, more and more reliance is placed on it. If a business needs a computer enough to buy it, then it should certainly need it enough to want to keep it running.

The surest way to get the computer running in the first place is to have it installed by the dealer – then he must assume responsibility for any installation problems. An early question for the dealer, therefore, is whether transportation and installation are included in the purchase price and, if not, what charge will be made for them.

From a maintenance point of view, it is also important to know the duration of the warranty on each item of equipment. Warranties vary from equipment to equipment and from dealer to dealer, so it may be prudent to search for the best combination of purchase price, warranty period and maintenance contract cost. It is certainly wise to procure maintenance contracts on all equipment and this is another factor which may be critical in the choice of a dealer. His initial purchase prices may be attractively low, but if he does not make a profit somehow he is sure to go out of business, so he may be charging excessively for maintenance contracts, or, worse, he may be saving on his maintenance organization and offering an inadequate service. In short, a dealer whose sales prices are excessively low may be one to avoid.

Maintenance contracts usually guarantee a **call-out time**, i.e. a time, after being called, within which the maintenance person will arrive at the user's premises. Different charges accompany different call-out times, and the user must decide which compromise suits him best. It is worth ensuring, however, that maintenance will be carried out on-site: removal of equipment from site results in added **down time** and uncertainty about the equipment's return. In some cases, equipment (e.g. certain types of disk) may have to be returned to contractors' premises for repair. Then the security of stored data would necessarily be compromised. If suitable agreements cannot be reached with the contractors, it may be preferable to destroy the faulty disk, depending on the level of confidentiality of the data.

Maintenance of a system is often thought of as an area where savings can be made. This is an imprudent attitude. However well a system operates at first, there is certain to come a time when a fault occurs – often due to the ineptitude of the operator. Then, however trivial the fault, assistance is likely to be required in rectifying it. If a business places reliance on a computer, it cannot afford not to make adequate provision for its maintenance.

In certain uses, it may not be acceptable to lose the computer when a fault occurs, even for a short time. Then, even the shortest call-out time is inadequate, and it may be necessary to have a duplicate computer in reserve. This, of course, adds to the cost of the system, but the spare computer can be put to work on other tasks while providing security for the main system. Redundancy can also be provided in the peripheral equipment if this is deemed necessary.

Even more important, it is essential to keep spare copies of up-to-date versions of all software, including important data, on magnetic tapes or disks. A computer fault can corrupt data, as can an operator's error, and more than one business has ceased trading because its computerized records were lost or corrupted. A minimum of two spare copies of software and data should be maintained, one on-site so as to be available for quick installation, and another off-site in case of an on-site catastrophe, such as fire. Both copies should be updated as often as is necessary to retain their usefulness.

Finally, operational staff require both training and documentation. Complete and understandable documentation should accompany all equipment and software and it is worth making sure that this will be the case.

Training can be expensive and it should be established at an early stage exactly how much will be necessary, how much it will cost, where it will take place (for travelling and accommodation can add significantly to the total cost), and what the training is expected to achieve. With changes in staff, further courses may be required, so it should be confirmed that these will continue to run for the foreseeable future. A limited future for courses usually implies that the equipment is obsolescent, and this is not what a purchaser should be seeking.

SUMMARY

In selecting a microcomputer system for anything but the simplest task, a purchaser who is not an expert will almost certainly require assistance from a computer salesman. However, salesmen themselves often possess inadequate knowledge, or have vested interests in selling certain types of equipment, so care needs to be exercised in choosing one.

The first step in securing the most appropriate system for the purpose in hand is to draw up, in writing, a comprehensive specification of requirements, which should detail the tasks which need to be performed.

While the requirements will influence the choice of hardware, they also determine the software and the latter will itself have a significant influence on the choice of hardware. In other words, hardware and software form an integrated system, each influencing the choice of the other, and neither should be chosen in isolation. Operating systems, database management systems, and applications software packages are all more efficient on certain computers than on others and, indeed, are not usable on some machines.

Hardware, too, needs to be planned carefully. Possible future enhancements, which may require more processing power, memory and terminal ports, should be considered. Peripheral equipment, such as printers and display units, should be chosen with reference to the specification of requirements and not with respect to bargain offers. Compatibility of the various items which comprise the system should be considered – for example, the most appropriate printer may not be compatible with the chosen processor. A full system demonstration by the salesman, prior to purchase, is an essential safeguard – though not a guarantee.

System and data security also need to be considered. Reliance on a computer may necessitate duplication of the system. Further, security of data files demands a method of duplicating them on secondary storage which is quick and easy.

Further considerations are transportation to site, installation, warranty, documentation, maintenance and training, both for operation and maintenance. Any or all of these may add to the total cost of the system, and it needs to be established with the dealer which of these items are excluded from the quoted price.

Modern microcomputers are relatively cheap and, in theory, easy to use. However, it is not always easy to choose the most appropriate system. Also, the total system is usually considerably more expensive than the price of a processor might suggest. If success is to be achieved, great care must be exercised in the purchase of the system.

Management of the use of the system is also important. Packaged systems can be handled by amateurs who stick to the rules. As knowledge of computers in general, and the system in use in particular, increases, so do the chances of successful operation. If that knowledge is applied out of its context, for example in attempting to develop rather than operate the system, disaster is likely. Software development is not as trivial as it may seem to an amateur with a smattering of knowledge, and this is often realized only after a project, enthusiastically and confidently begun, has come to grief, perhaps with the loss of a great deal of time and money.

PART II

HARDWARE, SOFTWARE AND PROCESSING

A course in computers. The sequence leads from an introduction to computer hardware, through the principles of software, to an explanation of processing.

CHAPTER 6

INTRODUCING COMPUTERS

A digital computer consists of **hardware** and **software** and is neither complete nor operational until these are both provided and functioning in harmony. Full understandings of the terms 'hardware' and 'software' will be developed in subsequent chapters, but at this point brief definitions are appropriate. Hardware consists of the tangible equipment which is the material fabric of a computer system. Software consists of the program instructions and data which are stored in the memory of the computer system.

All computers possess the same basic hardware features:

- storage for information;
- the ability to perform arithmetic and logic operations and execute stored instructions;
- a means of communication with the outside world.

Software comprises:

- **system software**, which renders the computer system operational and provides facilities for the user's convenience;
- **applications software**, which is purchased or written by the user to execute specific tasks.

The processing hardware consists only of two main functional components, a **processor** and a **memory**. The processor is capable of a limited number of simple and very basic operations which form the building blocks of all tasks that the computer can perform. The memory provides storage for the software – both program instructions and data. The processor is able to access all locations of the memory and operation consists of the processor acting in response to the contents of the memory. The computer is, therefore, a software-based system.

THE TWO GREAT STRENGTHS

One of the two major strengths of a general-purpose digital computer is its flexibility. It can perform any task that can be defined in a logical sequence of simple steps. These steps, in their particular sequence, form the algorithm of a given task. When translated into a computer language, they form the instructions which comprise a computer program. It is therefore the software which provides the computer's flexibility of application.

The essence of the software's flexibility is its ease of change. The instructions are stored in a computer in electronic hardware and are therefore electrically alterable. A program can thus easily be corrected, extended or modified, for any reason, which makes it an attractive alternative to designing a wholly hardware circuit to perform the same task. (This is true in theory, since it is easy to make changes to software. It is notoriously difficult to get the changes correct, so the ease of change provides scope for error.) Moreover, when the computer has completed one task, the same memory is used to store the instructions and data for another.

Hardware, on the other hand, offers both the stable structure of the system and the electronic circuitry for the storage and processing of the software. The second great strength of a computer is its speed of operation, which is provided by the electronic hardware.

WHY COMPUTERS?

It is customary to think of a computer as solving a problem. We hear such remarks as 'Wait while I ask the computer' and 'I'll get the computer to solve it'. However, in performing any task, the computer is merely following a sequence of instructions with which it has been programmed. It does this faithfully, with perfect accuracy, for it is incapable of anything else; if the results are inaccurate, the fault will almost certainly lie in the data, or in the logic of the instructions rather than their execution by the computer.

Consequently, if a problem is to be solved, the programmer must put into the computer a definition of the solution, or of a way of arriving at the solution. This may sound strange and questions may be asked such as 'Why do we need the computer to solve a problem if the programmer himself can solve it?' and 'Wouldn't it be quicker for the programmer to solve the problem, anyway, instead of taking the time to program the computer to do so?'. The reasons for using the computer lie in its two great strengths: speed and flexibility.

It is clearly not worth spending an hour writing a program to solve a problem which can be solved by hand in ten minutes. However, if the process is to be repeated, perhaps hundreds of times, for different sets of data, then it is well worth having a program which can be used on each occasion. The computer software's flexibility allows the same program to be used for different inputs of data and the hardware's speed makes it ideal for carrying out repetitive tasks. The same procedure is followed each time, but the deduced results and thus the output are, on each occasion, appropriate to the input data. An example of this type of repetitive procedure is the production of a firm's weekly or monthly pay slips.

Then there are problems, such as the mathematical equations involved in meteorological forecasting, which would take a human many years to solve – rendering the results worthless. Knowing the method, however, he can program a computer to carry out the solutions and, once this is done, the computer's speed allows results to be obtained in a matter of hours.

Indeed, the number of applications of computers is enormous and many were mentioned in Part I. It was also shown that all computers are not equally suitable for particular tasks. They cover a wide range, from the smallest micros to the largest mainframes, and these display capabilities according to their design and in proportion to their cost. Nevertheless, their principles of operation are common and it is these principles which are the subject of the next eight chapters.

CHAPTER 7

HARDWARE

Essentially, a digital computer is an arithmetic and logical calculator provided with access to extensive storage, the facility for input and output communication and the ability, provided by a software operating system, to optimize the efficiency of its own operation.

Modern micro systems are often packages so that peripheral equipment, such as floppy disks and input terminals are contained in the samc housing as the computer itself. This makes it difficult, at a superficial level, to identify what a computer actually is. This chapter attempts to do this.

OVERVIEW

For a machine to be a computer, it must possess the means of executing certain arithmetic and logical operations. For this purpose the **arithmetic logic unit** (ALU) is provided. A computer must also have the logic for interpreting software instructions which provide the information for determining what operations are to be performed and in what order. This logic forms the **control unit**. Further, it must possess **memory** or **storage** to contain the data on which the operations are to be performed, the programs which contain the operating instructions, and the results of the operations. Finally, since the computer's purpose is to function on behalf of human users, it must possess the means of communicating with them. **Input** and **output devices** are therefore necessary.

These four functions form the basis of every general purpose digital computer. They are illustrated in Figure 7.1, where the dotted lines show the direction of control signals,

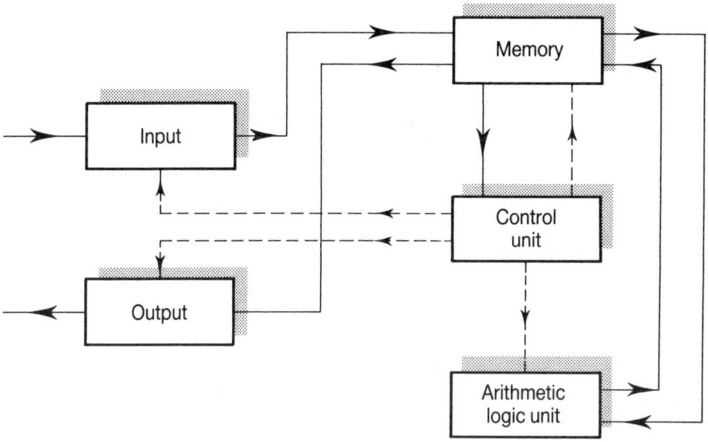

Figure 7.1 *Essential functional modules of a digital computer.*

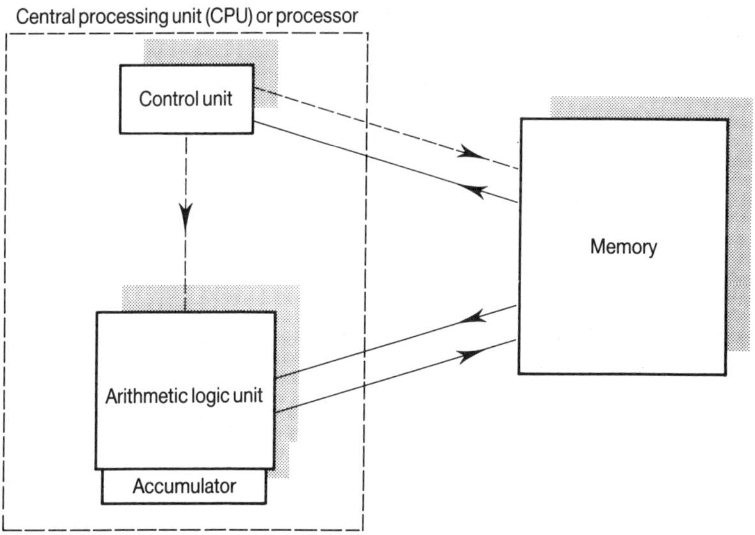

Figure 7.2 *Central processing unit (CPU) within the computer.*

which always emanate from the control unit, and the heavy lines show the directions of transfer of data and/or program instructions.

The area of the computer in which the real work, or **processing**, is carried out is the **central processing unit** (CPU). This consists of the ALU and the control unit (see Figure 7.2) and usually includes some memory of its own. In general, therefore, a computer consists of a processor, additional memory, and the ability to communicate with the outside world via input/output (I/O) devices. In recent years, however, the terms 'processor' and 'computer' have often been used synonymously, particularly with reference to micro equipment, though this is not correct.

A **microprocessor**, consisting of arithmetic and control units and some storage, can now be purchased on a single **chip**. To make a computer of it, an I/O device and, usually, more storage must be provided. However, processors can be used on their own – when only limited external communication is needed. An example of such a use is the control of a domestic appliance such as a washing machine. A program, defining the control process, is stored in the memory of the microprocessor chip and, since signals are exchanged only between the processor and the washing machine, no I/O devices are required for communication with the outside world – except very basic and limited user controls.

THE CONTROL UNIT

The control unit is the administrative centre of the computer. Its logic considers the software instructions in sequence, determines what actions they demand, and initiates these actions by sending control signals to the ALU, memory and input and output devices (see the dotted lines in Figure 7.1).

The control unit knows, from the software instructions, when information should be input to the computer. It sends start and stop signals to the appropriate input device, and it controls the transfer of the information incoming to the memory. It controls the output of information in a similar way. It tells the ALU what operations to perform and when to perform them, where in memory to find the data for the operations, and where in memory to store the results.

It should be recognized, however, that the control unit has no inherent knowledge of its own. Its ability is to interpret program instructions, and it deduces what actions are required only from the software stored in the computer's memory (see Chapter 14 for a description of processing).

The Arithmetic Logic Unit

The arithmetic logic unit (ALU) is the site where all computations are carried out. It consists of electronic logic circuitry capable of arithmetic and logical functions. Examples of arithmetic functions are addition, subtraction, multiplication and division. Examples of logical functions are the AND and OR functions, which are explained in the Glossary.

Since all processes of computation can be reduced to a small number of such elementary arithmetic and logical functions, a computer provided with a well chosen selection of them will possess great flexibility and be suitable for a wide range of applications. This is the basis of the design of a 'general-purpose' computer.

Close to the ALU there are a number of **registers** which provide temporary storage for data which is being operated on. A register is a device designed to store a defined amount of data, usually a word, or a number of bytes (see Chapter 8 for definitions of these terms). A particularly important register is the **accumulator** which is the location where the results of calculations (such as addition and subtraction) are formed.

Input/Output (I/O) Units

The most common modern means of I/O are the terminal keyboard on which to input instructions and data and the **visual display unit** (VDU) on which to receive output. Many computer users, particularly of microcomputers, require no more than these. A permanent visual record of output, however, demands the use of a **printer** which prints output onto paper.

Traditional methods of input were by punched cards and punched paper tape, though these are almost obsolete, having largely been superseded by direct keyboard input.

Information has also traditionally been output to **bulk**

storage devices such as magnetic tapes and magnetic disks (which are discussed in Chapter 9). Data on such storage media cannot be read directly by a human being: it must be passed back through a computer and transferred to a printer or VDU. However, the portability of disks, particularly **floppy disks,** and tapes makes them convenient as output devices from a computer, secure as permanent storage devices, and easy to use at some later time as input devices to the same or another computer.

For graphical information, the **graph plotter** provides a direct means of output, and **touch-screen** technology offers an easy method of input. There are a number of ways in which touch-screen is engineered, but the result of all of them is that the touch of a finger, or in some cases a specially designed device, such as a **light pen**, on the screen is sensed and the coordinates of the point of contact recorded. Instructions embodied in a program, or from the user via the keyboard, determine how the information is used.

Graphical input can also be achieved by the **mouse** and the **joystick**, both of which are directly connected to the terminal and which, when moved by hand, cause the movement of a cursor on the screen. The mouse is moved freely in a horizontal plane while the joystick is a lever with freedom of movement in two dimensions.

As to the future, research is progressing into **voice recognition** and it is expected that both voice input and output will be commonplace in the not too distant future.

MEMORY

In the earliest days of electronic computing, memory was used only for storing the data which the computer was going to need while executing a single program. The operator, who was also the programmer, knew the location of each item of data in the memory and the program included instructions for the data's retrieval prior to its use. The program itself was run as it was loaded into the machine, each instruction being taken directly into the central processing unit and executed.

It was then realized that since data and program instructions took the same form within the computer, the memory that could store the one could store the other. Clearly if the largest programs were to be stored within the machine, the computer had to be furnished with a large supply of memory, but until recently memory has been a very expensive commodity. It has therefore been one of the most researched aspects of computer hardware, many technologies having been used in the search for miniaturization, cost reduction, faster access and greater security.

Modern computing is heavily dependent on storage. Indeed it is based on storage and the handling of stored information, and the importance of memory cannot be overstated. It will therefore be discussed at length in the next two chapters.

CHAPTER 8

MEMORY

There are two main categories of memory. **Computer memory**, or **primary storage**, is a part of the computer and is necessary for storing the programs being executed and their data. It normally consists of **random access memory** (RAM). **Secondary storage** (the subject of the next chapter), also referred to as **backing store, bulk storage** or **auxiliary storage**, is cheaper than RAM and is used to store programs and data not in immediate use. It generally consists of **hard disks, floppy disks** or **magnetic tapes** and, since these exist outside the computer, it takes much longer to access secondary storage than it does to access primary storage. A great deal of time would therefore be wasted if the computer had to retrieve instructions and items of data from secondary storage at the time of executing them. It is therefore arranged, within a computer, for programs and data which are being held in secondary storage to be transferred into primary storage prior to their processing.

THE NATURE OF STORAGE

Computer storage is available on a number of media and in various technologies, but is always based on the fact that a single storage element can exist in one of two states and can therefore be used to represent a binary digit. In other words, if it is in one state it is considered to represent '0' (zero) and, if in its other possible state, to represent '1' (one). The represented binary digit is known as a **bit.**

Computing depends on stringing a number of binary bits together to form a **binary code** with which to represent numeric, alphabetic and other characters. Each type of computer is designed to respond to instructions in its own code and to operate on a given number of bits strung together, i.e. on its own computer **word** (see Figure 8.1). Storage in a **fixed-word computer** is therefore arranged so that a word, rather than a bit, is operated on as an entity. This means that if the contents of one word are to be transferred to another, the bits are all transferred in parallel rather than one after the other. Clearly, for some functions, such as the transfer of large quantities of data from one file to another, greater speed of operation can be achieved by using a machine with a larger word size. Typical word sizes for larger computers are between 20 and 60 bits. The most frequent word size of micro-computers has increased from 8 to 16 bits, though 32-bit machines are now becoming common.

Most modern computers have greater flexibility of storage than fixed-word machines. They are **byte-addressable** and even bit-addressable, as well as word-addressable. A byte is a subset of a word (see Figure 8.1) and its length is designated by the computer manufacturer, although usage has decreed that a byte is now commonly understood to consist of eight bits. In a byte-addressable machine, any byte or word in storage can be separately addressed. Bit-addressing adds the facility of accessing any bit individually.

RANDOM ACCESS MEMORY

For a computer to function at an efficient speed, information must be accessible from memory at a rate comparable to that of the operation of the computer's logic circuitry. Any item of

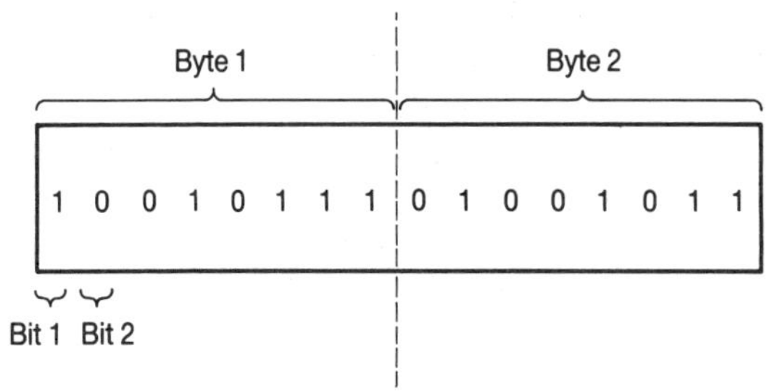

Figure 8.1 *Example of a 16-bit computer word consisting of two 8-bit bytes.*

information, whether it is data or a program instruction, must therefore be retrievable from storage as readily and quickly as any other – if the computer is not to be hesitant in its operation. This places the criterion on primary storage, in which the operational program and its data are held, that any one storage location is as quickly accessible as any other. The memory within the computer which meets this criterion is therefore referred to as random access memory (RAM).

There have been several technologies used in the provision of RAM, but three are prevalent today. First, older computers may possess **core store** in which the storage elements consist of tiny ferrite cores which can be magnetized in one of two directions, these being used to represent one or other of the binary digits.

The second type of RAM in use is **bubble memory**. This, like core store, is magnetic memory, but it does not consist of discrete memory elements. It is a solid-state device, with data being stored in tiny **magnetic domains**, or **bubbles**, fabricated onto the surface of a wafer of garnet. It is high density storage, with a unit providing 1 Mbit or more. Access to it is not as fast as to semiconductor memory (see below), but it holds the possibility of providing bulk storage for smaller systems, i.e. below 30–50 Mbits of storage. Then, fast access RAM would be provided by semiconductor memory and secondary storage by bubble memory (which is also RAM), thus obviating the need for the much slower access disks and magnetic tapes. It is yet to be seen whether this possibility becomes a reality.

Current computers, however, are mainly supplied with **semiconductor store**, in which huge numbers of storage elements are etched into the circuitry of a single silicon chip. This has reduced both the size and the cost of storage, and allowed computers to have access to increased amounts of RAM.

Under the general heading of 'semiconductor technology', there are several sub-sets. Over the years new types of logic, smaller or faster or both, have emerged. It is therefore possible to get semiconductor storage with different speeds of access. Cost is proportional to speed, however, so it is often found that the majority of RAM in a computer is composed of a cheaper range of storage while small special stores, reserved for the ALU and control unit, are made up of a faster variety.

A consideration for RAM is whether or not the type of storage is **volatile,** i.e. whether the contents of the store are lost when the electric power supply is removed. Core store and bubble memory are non-volatile, but semiconductor storage is, in general, volatile. Data which needs to be retained must be **dumped** from volatile RAM to non-volatile secondary storage at regular intervals as a precaution against the possibility of power failure.

ADDRESSING

Information arriving in the computer must be stored prior to its use and must be retrievable. The machine must therefore have a means of **addressing** its storage locations.

The storage in a computer can be likened in two dimensions to a rack of pigeon-holes, or letter boxes (see Figure 8.2), each defined by a number, or address. In computing, numbering always commences at zero rather than one, and this is reflected in the addresses of the locations in the figure. Since the contents are **written in** or **read out** electrically, each location is accessed via wires over which electric pulses are transmitted. When reading or writing is to be carried out, the necessary address is interpreted by the computer's logic circuitry so that currents are supplied to the appropriate wires for accessing that location. In this sense, a location is not

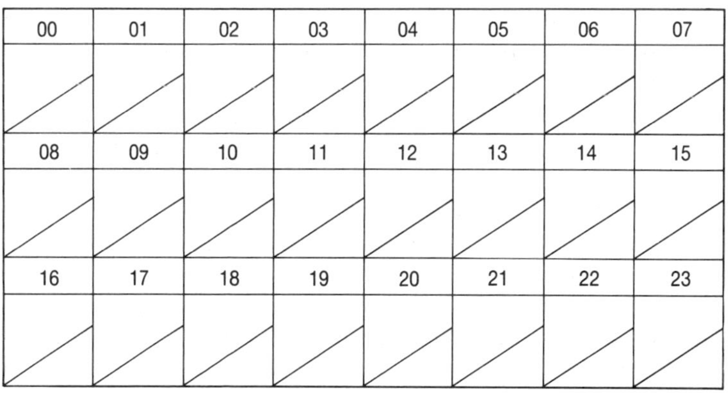

Figure 8.2 *A storage array can be likened to a rack of pigeon-holes.*

necessarily a single bit or storage element, but depends on the design of the computer. It may be a bit, byte or word, as previously described.

In writing into memory, electrical pulses are sent so as to set the memory elements of the required address to the necessary values (0 or 1). In reading from memory, the values of the memory elements of the address are sensed and transmitted to the required destination – control unit, arithmetic unit or another memory location.

For the computer's logic to interpret the address of the location to be accessed, it must be stored in a register known as the **address register**. The number of locations which can be addressed directly therefore depends on the size of the address register. In general, if it consists of N elements, or binary bits, it can uniquely address 2^N locations. For example, a machine with a 16-bit address register can have 2^{16} or 65 536 (referred to as 64K) directly addressable RAM locations.

Until recently, it was usual for a computer's address register size and its word size to be the same. Now, however, with RAM being miniaturized and less expensive, it has become practical and economic to provide larger amounts of RAM. With increasing demands being made on information processing, many computers, including micros, are being provided with address registers larger than the computer's word size. This, of course, increases the machine's addressing capability.

Most computer applications, however, require an even greater volume of storage than this and the deficiency must be made good with the use of secondary storage. An efficient way of managing this, to give the impression of expanded RAM, is by the use of the principle of **virtual storage**.

VIRTUAL STORAGE

When a program is first read into a machine which employs virtual storage, the computer's operating system recognizes that the program is too large for the RAM and stores some parts of it in RAM and some parts in secondary storage. In doing so it retains records of the addresses in the RAM storage locations (known as 'real addresses') as well as addresses for the parts of the program in secondary storage (known as 'virtual addresses'). At run-time the virtual addresses are decoded and those parts of the program are transferred into RAM in blocks, or segments, so that each block is in the main memory when it is due to be processed and continuous execution takes place. This is a function of the **operating system** (see Chapter 11) and is therefore not something which ordinary computer users can control or are aware of.

The process allows programmers to write programs without having to consider the size of memory of the computers on which they may be run. However, provision of this facility adds complexity and thus cost to the operating system. Virtual storage is an accepted facility on mainframes and minis, but it is not yet a function of the operating systems of micros. However, the technique is built into some proprietary software packages, such as word processors, which employ it when handling large documents.

READ ONLY MEMORY

While RAM is generally volatile, there are some types of semiconductor memory which are not. These allow ready access to the information stored in them but usually require a specified technique and a much longer time for writing to them. They are therefore referred to as **read only memory** (ROM) and are used for protecting the information stored in them from being over-written by other data. In some cases the memory pattern representing the program to be stored is written into the ROM during manufacture.

Until recently it has not been possible to alter ROM while it is *in situ*. This development has been achieved via an evolutionary path and there are a number of categories of ROM, these being defined by the manner in which the ROM may be altered.

Programmable read only memory (PROM) may allow a stored program to be added to in the sense that binary 0s may be changed to 1s, but it does not permit the reverse of the process. This is because the method of creating 1s is destructive of certain aspects of the memory elements, usually tiny fuses, which are then unalterable.

Some PROMs are erasable, but not under normal conditions. **Erasable programmable read only memory**

(EPROM) allows re-programming after the stored information has been erased, usually by prolonged exposure of the memory to ultra-violet light.

More recently, the **electrically erasable programmable read only memory** (EEPROM) has been developed. This offers the EPROM's advantage of a re-programmable ROM, while eliminating the disadvantage of having to remove the device from the system in order to erase it. The EEPROM can be erased electrically while *in situ*.

In general, PROMs are used not only for protecting information within the computer from being over-written, but also for the transfer of stored information. Being non-volatile and manufactured on microchips, they are portable and provide the medium for the sale and transportation of many software packages – such as system software, educational packages and games. They can simply be purchased and plugged into an area of the computer's memory which, during manufacture, is reserved for the purpose.

PARITY CHECKS

There are many ways in which data within a computer can be lost or corrupted, the three most usual being operator error, system failure and lack of foresight in application program design. This last is manifested in such ways as allowing data areas in store to be over-written before the data in them has been dumped to secondary storage.

With these exceptions, data in store is secure; it will not suffer spontaneous corruption. However, when data is being transferred from one area of the computer to another, or to/from secondary storage, there is a very small chance (about one in several million) that a single bit may be corrupted. The reversal of a 1 to 0 or a 0 to 1 can be highly significant and, though its probability is low, the number of instructions which can be processed in a second by a computer make it likely to occur within a finite time. It is therefore well worth guarding against.

The method employed is known as **parity checking** and this is built into all computers. The principle is that the number of bits defined by the machine's binary code for representing a transferable entity (a word, byte or character) is increased by one to include a **parity bit** and this is set to 1 or 0, as necessary to ensure that the number of 1s in the code is an even number (for **even parity**) or an odd number (for **odd parity**). The examples below show a six-bit code with the parity bit (P) being set for even parity.

Bit	1	2	3	4	5	P
	0	1	1	0	1	1
	1	0	1	1	1	0

Whenever data is transferred, it is checked on receipt for correctness within whichever parity convention is in use in the computer. If the number of 1s in the entity does not conform to the expected odd or even parity, retransmission is requested. This is repeated up to a predetermined number of times, after which the machine outputs an error message indicating a permanent fault. Clearly, if two bits in an entity are corrupted, the entity will exhibit the correct parity and single bit parity checking will not reveal the error. However, with the probability of a single error being exceedingly small, that of more than one is infinitesimally tiny.

Single bit parity checking does not detect which bit has been corrupted, but it is an invaluable test for correctness. Since it is carried out at each data transfer within the computer, it constitutes an overhead in processing. In the interest of achieving reliable computing and accurate results, this is an essential aspect of the machine's **housekeeping** overheads.

In some cases double bit parity checking is used. Then more elaborate tests, in accordance with mathematical formulae, are applied, and these allow more accurate diagnostic information to be deduced about the actual error.

CHAPTER 9
SECONDARY STORAGE

Secondary storage is bulk storage provided outside the computer. As it is not part of the machine's internal memory, it is not directly addressable as RAM and its access time is therefore considerably longer than that of the computer's own RAM. Its advantages, however, are that it is cheap and non-volatile. Its purposes are to:

- store programs not currently in use;
- store data which will be used or which has been calculated or collected by the computer;
- form a **security dump** for such data;
- provide security stores, both on and away from the computer site, for programs, in case of their destruction within the computer (because of catastrophe, power failure, or corruption due to a fault);
- provide a means of transporting software, in the form of programs or data, from one computer to another, perhaps with long or short term storage in transit.

The best known type of secondary storage is the floppy disk, as this is prevalent in microcomputer systems and is familiar in the office as an integral part of word processors. Other forms of secondary storage are hard disks, magnetic tape and, only recently, optical disks. When any form of secondary storage is provided, it forms a part of the computer system, but it is not a part of the computer itself and its hardware is referred to as a **computer peripheral**. It should be added, however, that many microcomputers are now constructed with a floppy disk handler or **disk drive**, not as a distinct peripheral, but as an integral part of the computer housing itself.

MAGNETIC TAPE

Magnetic tape for computer storage is like that for tape recorders in its principle of operation. It is usually half an inch wide and 2400 feet long. It consists of a reel of plastic tape with a coating of ferrous oxide which can be magnetized by passing it over a magnetizing head. Once the information has been recorded onto the tape in the form of magnetized bits on the ferrous oxide, it remains there until it is over-written by re-recording – or until the ferrous oxide coating wears away through use.

Data is stored on the tape in the form of binary bits which are magnetized in rows across the tape and tracks along the length of the tape (see Figure 9.1). The usual standard is nine-track tape, which means that each row consists of nine bits. The distance between the rows determines the **packing density** of data on the tape, which is usually measured in **bits per inch** (bpi). Typical figures are between 1500 and 6000 bpi. The tape speed, or the speed of movement of the tape across the read or

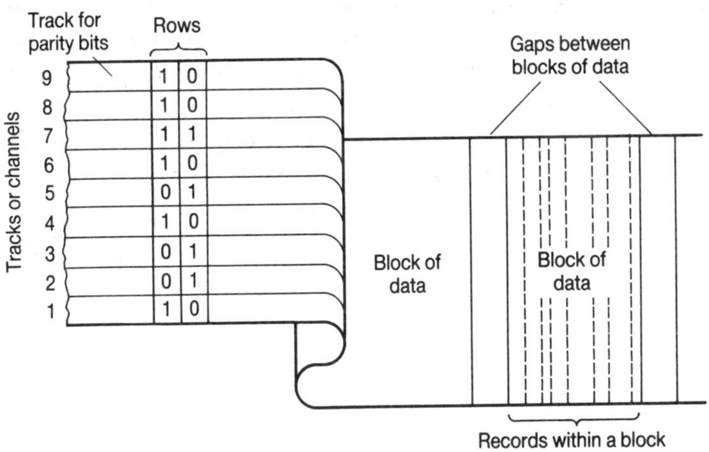

Figure 9.1 *Data storage on magnetic tape.*

write head, is quoted in inches per second (ips), typical speeds being between 75 and 200 ips. The combination of this and the packing density determines the **data transfer rate**. This is the rate at which data is transferred to or from the tape, and is usually quoted in thousands of bits per second or kilobits per second (Kbit/sec). Typical figures for this are 200–1200 kilobits per second.

Magnetic tape is cheap and very convenient for long term storage in archives. In use, its disadvantage is its slowness of access since data can only be found by a sequential search. Achieving the most effective use of tape storage requires careful design of the data format, based on a knowledge of the inefficiencies of tape handling and the purpose for which the data is to be used. Formatting consists of compiling the data into **records** and then storing numbers of related records together in **blocks**, with each block being given a unique header. Access to an individual item of data therefore involves a sequential search of **block headers** for the right block, a search within the block itself for the appropriate record and, finally, a search for the data item itself.

The method of accessing the data on the tape is therefore seen to be **serial access**. For example, the hundredth block on the tape can only be reached and read after the first 99 have been passed. The time to wind forward and back is considerable compared with the time to read data from RAM.

Cassettes and cartridges of magnetic tape are also common to microcomputer users. Non-erasable (read only) cartridges are the medium on which many pre-written programs and computer games are sold, and are plugged into the memory area of the micro as required.

MAGNETIC DISKS

Magnetic disks offer much faster data access than magnetic tape. They are cylindrical and are similar in principle to a gramophone record, in that the information is stored in tracks on the surface and that reading and writing are carried out while the disk rotates about its central axis at a predetermined constant speed. However, whereas a record possesses a single spiralling track, a disk possesses a number of individual circular tracks. Further, whereas reading from a record is dependent on the mechanical movements of a stylus, that from a disk is carried out electrically by lowering a magnetic head very close to the track so as to detect the magnetized information stored there – like passing a magnetic tape over a head. For a **hard disk**, the head rides on a cushion of air a fraction of a millimetre above the surface of the disk; for a **floppy disk**, which consists of a plastic cylinder covered with a magnetic coating, the head actually touches the surface. A floppy disk is thus subject to wear – like magnetic tape.

Disks are classified as **fixed head** or **moving head**. In the former the head does not move across the disk but only towards or away from the track – the disk drive thus requiring a magnetic head for each track. In moving head disk drives, a head accesses more than one track (but not necessarily all the tracks on the disk) and must therefore also move across the disk.

In some cases, disks are single platters (see Figure 9.2) – as floppy disks are – but most hard disks come as **stacks**, a stack consisting of a number of individual disks, each accessed by its own heads (see Figure 9.3). This clearly increases storage capacity, particularly as data may be stored on both sides of each individual disk. A fixed stack is immovable from within

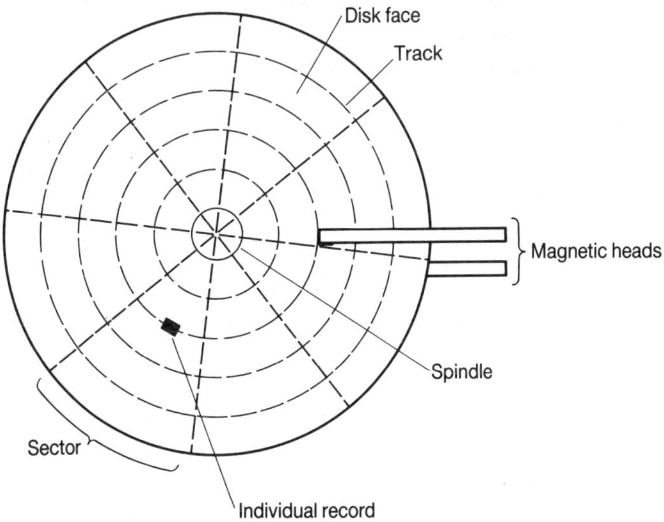

Figure 9.2 *Data storage on a magnetic disk.*

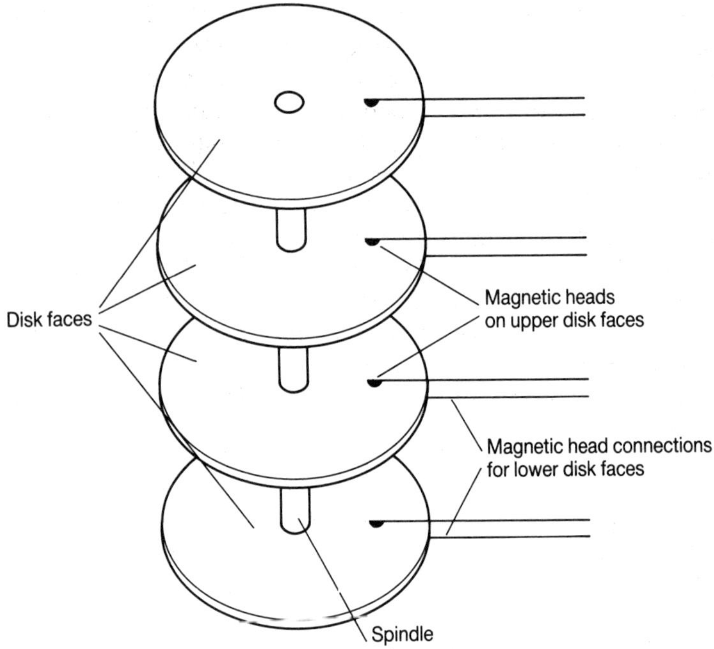

Figure 9.3 *Disk stack with magnetic heads.*

its drive, but most stacks are **removable disk packs**. They can be exchanged so as to archive or transport the information stored on them, while new storage capacity is provided to the computer system as a whole.

Disk access is **direct access** in that the required data can be accessed directly without having first to read the records before it, as in accessing serial access tape. Direct access depends on the disk storage being segregated into locations, addressable in terms of which disk in the pack the location is on, which face of the disk, which track on the face, and which segment of the track (see Figure 9.2). However, although disk access is often referred to as random, this is incorrect since there are two variable times involved in accessing data. The **seek time** is the time taken for a movable head to be positioned over the required track. The **rotational time** is the time for the disk to circumscribe a partial revolution until the item of data required is under the head. The **access time** is the sum of the seek and rotational times.

Disk capacity is usually quoted in bytes, and ranges from less than a million bytes (megabytes or Mbytes) for some floppies to over a billion bytes for some hard disk packs. Transfer rates range up to about three megabytes per second.

Disks are a true example of precision engineering and, as a result, they have in the past required a controlled environment, primarily in the form of a level base and dust-free atmosphere. These necessities have recently been overcome in some measure. Many microcomputers use floppy disks without reference to a horizontal base, and even on the move. Moreover, the **Winchester** technology, in which disk packs containing their own heads are vacuum sealed, avoids the possibility of dust or grit causing damage to the heads or disk surfaces. Positioning the disk in its drive makes electrical connections which not only supply power for rotation but also provide a communication path to the heads.

Clearly disks offer faster access and greater general flexibility than magnetic tapes, but tapes have the advantage of being considerably cheaper for mass storage.

Optical Disk Storage

The most recent development in secondary storage is the optical disk. The disk itself is metallic, but storage is not achieved by magnetizing the surface. Rather, reading and writing both depend on the use of laser beams. To write a bit of data to the disk, a laser beam is focused on a predetermined point and the heat generated causes the formation of a gas in a polymer layer under the surface. This pushes up on the metal surface layer, forming a bubble. The data storage is thus beneath the metallic surface of the disk and is protected from physical wear. Reading is achieved by a low powered laser detecting whether a bubble exists or not. The process of forming a bubble is irreversible, so optical storage is non-erasable – at least at the present stage of the technology.

Due to the precision with which a laser beam may be focused, tracks can be closer together than on a magnetic disk, as can the bits along a track (the bubbles). The storage density of an optical disk is therefore at least ten times greater than that of magnetic disks.

Since the laser beam can be focused from a relatively large

distance, there is no need for the equivalent of a magnetic head to be in close proximity with the disk. This reduces the chance of the head crashing onto the disk and damaging it, as can happen with magnetic disks. It also facilities disk removal. Further advantages of optical disks are lower power consumption, a lower overall cost per byte of storage and small physical size.

It is expected that optical disks, with their very high storage capacities, will be very suitable for filing the vast amounts of historic, non-alterable, data (such as text, coloured pictures and voice recordings) required in office and commercial environments.

CHAPTER 10

LEVELS OF COMPUTER LANGUAGE

A computer consists of hardware and software and is neither complete nor operational until these are both provided and functioning in harmony. All computers possess the same basic hardware features:

- storage for information,
- the ability to perform arithmetic operations and execute stored instructions in a sequential manner,
- a means of communication with the outside world.

Software comprises:

- **system software**, which renders the computer system operational and provides facilities for the user's convenience,
- **applications software**, which is purchased or written by the user to execute specific tasks.

Those were the words which began Part II and the hardware features referred to above have already been described. This chapter and the following two will describe the fundamentals of the software which commonly comprises the system software of a computer system. The development of software has been closely linked to the evolution of computer language and such a discussion must commence with a review of the different levels of language.

MACHINE LANGUAGE

In our decimal number system, ten different states (0–9) can be represented by a single digit. To represent a number greater than nine, one or more further digits are required (e.g. 10, 89, 364, 2016). The electronic devices on which computers are based are **binary** – they can each represent only two states – and are thus incapable of representing the decimal numbering system directly. An everyday analogy is the light bulb, which is either OFF or ON. Such a device when used as the basis for a numbering system, can be said to represent 0 or 1. To represent higher numbers, further binary digits (and therefore devices) are required. Table 10.1 shows the principle and it can be seen that to represent the decimal digit 9, four binary digits (1001) are necessary, or four devices in the sequence of ON, OFF, OFF, ON.

Since the devices on which computers are based are binary, the methods of storage and communication within a computer are in binary forms. The various binary code systems created by the computer manufacturers to fulfil the needs of their machines are **machine languages** or **machine codes**. In particular, they must not only encode information for representation, but also provide the means of building series of binary codes which a particular machine's circuitry interprets as instructions.

Machine languages consist of strings of zeros and ones, but are not limited to representing numerics. Much of the information processed by computers consists of text, so alphabetic characters, punctuation marks, etc., must all have individual codes. This is not a new concept. Morse Code is an example of a binary language; it represents all the above mentioned types of characters by sequences of two symbols, dots and dashes.

In the early days of computing all programs were written in machine language. There was no intermediate stage between man and machine, and the programmer had to specify the location within the machine's storage where every instruction and every item of data should be held. Thereafter he had to refer to these, precisely, when he wished to carry out operations. Writing large programs and manipulating data were formidable tasks, and since all instructions consisted only of sequences of binary digits, programs were difficult to read, test or amend.

Table 10.1 *Binary representation of decimal numbers.*

Decimal number	*Binary representation*	*Electrical equivalent (four devices)*			
0	0	OFF	OFF	OFF	OFF
1	1	OFF	OFF	OFF	ON
2	10	OFF	OFF	ON	OFF
3	11	OFF	OFF	ON	ON
4	100	OFF	ON	OFF	OFF
5	101	OFF	ON	OFF	ON
6	110	OFF	ON	ON	OFF
7	111	OFF	ON	ON	ON
8	1000	ON	OFF	OFF	OFF
9	1001	ON	OFF	OFF	ON
10	1010	ON	OFF	ON	OFF
11	1011	ON	OFF	ON	ON
12	1100	ON	ON	OFF	OFF
13	1101	ON	ON	OFF	ON
14	1110	ON	ON	ON	OFF
15	1111	ON	ON	ON	ON

ASSEMBLY LANGUAGE

Assembly languages were developed to overcome the difficulties of programming in machine language. An assembly language consists of a set of **mnemonic** codes, symbolic of the binary instructions which they represent. It permits the programmer to function in a manner akin to the computer's mode of operation, while avoiding having to work exclusively in binary code.

It should be remembered, however, that this symbolic language is for the programmer's convenience and the computer can still only operate and communicate in binary code. Therefore, before an assembly language program can be run, a means of translating it from assembly language to machine language is required. This takes the form of a special program, written to cater for all the possible codes in the given assembly language, called an **assembler**.

For convenience, some assembly languages contain single codes which convert into several machine language instructions, but usually the assembler translates instructions from the assembly language **source program** into instructions in the machine language **object program** on a one-to-one ratio. This implies that the usual inefficiency which occurs in any translation process will not be introduced by assembly, and a well written assembly language program will be efficient in its use of both storage and CPU time.

Once the complete object program has been assembled, it can be stored and run again and again, thus saving the time taken for assembly on each occasion of its use. However, if the source program is changed in any way, it must be re-assembled.

To illustrate the nature of assembly language instructions, consider the following typical sequence. The instructions are on the left of the delineating character, '/', and comments are on the right of it. (The accumulator is at the heart of the processor within the computer and is the location, or register, in which the results of calculations are formed – see Chapter 7.)

```
CLA    / Zeroize (or clear) accumulator
ADD A/ Add contents of address A to accumulator
SUB B  / Subtract contents of address B from accumulator
STO C / Store contents of accumulator in address C
```

The above instructions carry out a simple subtraction, having first cleared the accumulator, setting the value of its contents to zero, to avoid corruption by data stored for earlier calculations. The final instruction transfers the result to a chosen address (C) for storage, since the accumulator will be required again for the next calculation. It should also be noted that to make this section of program possible, the programmer may previously have had to designate the addresses A, B and C in storage, and also to have arranged for A and B to contain the values required.

A feature of assembly language is that the programmer can insert comments in the program, as in the example, to assist in understanding it at a later date. A **delineating character** ('/' above) is used to separate comment from instruction. The assembler does not translate anything on the same line following this delineating character, so comments do not affect the machine language program (the object program) produced by the assembler.

The result of direct correspondence between assembly and machine languages is that the programmer still needs to know and control every aspect of the storage and manipulation, within the computer, of the instructions and data. He needs to think like the computer – one step at a time at machine level. For this reason, assembly language, like machine language, is referred to as **low level language**. A further disadvantage of assembly language is that programs are specific to the type of machine for which the assembler is written. They are not **portable** to other computers.

HIGH LEVEL LANGUAGE

High level languages (HLLs) isolate the programmer from the operation of the computer. They consist of statements in readable form and thus allow the programmer to concentrate more on the problem for which he is writing the program, and less on the step-by-step functioning of the hardware. Nor does he need to know the locations in which his instructions and data are stored. An HLL instruction translates into more than one machine language instruction (typically between two and eight). Because there is not a direct, one-to-one correspondence, as in the translation of assembly language, there may be some loss of efficiency in translation. (Again it is emphasized that the computer itself can only function in the binary code of machine language.)

The program for the translation of the HLL source program into the machine language object program is called a **compiler** – though sometimes an **interpreter** is used (see pp. 92 and 98). A compiler is more elaborate in its operation than an assembler, though it performs a comparable function. Like an assembler's object program, the compiler's object program is compiled in its entirety prior to being run, and can therefore be stored for future use. This can save a great deal of processing time when the program is run again, particularly in large systems where compilation can be lengthy. While performing its translation function, a compiler checks the source code for syntactical errors to ensure that the HLL has been used in accordance with its grammar and that no logical ambiguities exist in the object code.

As an illustration of HLL code, consider the following typical sequence of instructions.

IF *Y* IS GREATER THAN 10 THEN
(LET) $X = Y - Z$
ELSE (LET) $X = Y + Z$

Not only is an algebraic expression being evaluated without the programmer being aware of the computer's process of achieving this, but the program also contains the basis for the decision of which expression to evaluate. And all this is specified in three lines of code. A typical number of machine language instructions generated by the compiler to achieve this is about eight.

The need to make the above decision introduces a logical branch in the program. When the program is being run, only one leg of the branch will be taken, depending on the value of *Y*. Such conditional branching is one way in which software provides the flexibility offered by a computer to its users. The syntax of high level languages facilitates programming of conditional branching, but it is also necessary and possible in all other levels of language.

An HLL achieves programming efficiencies in many ways. It results in programs which are easy to write, read, test, correct and expand; it allows faster programming; it permits someone with a knowledge only of the problem and the given HLL, but not of the computer hardware, to be a programmer. It also, in theory at least, allows portability of programs from one machine to another. In practice, computer manufacturers undermine this great advantage by introducing modifications and extensions into the standard definitions of languages for use on their machines, so that compilers need to be specifically written (or modified) for use on a given computer.

Examples of HLLs are:

- FORTRAN which is designed for scientific work,
- COBOL which is designed for commercial programming,
- PL/1 which has attempted to include the best qualities of each of these,

- BASIC which is simple and similar to FORTRAN and is currently a very popular choice for programming microcomputers,
- Pascal which was one of the earliest HLLs for which a compiler was available on micros,
- CHILL which has been developed to include special facilities essential to communications programming.

FOURTH GENERATION LANGUAGES

The high level languages discussed above (now often referred to as Third Generation Languages) abstract the programmer from the operation of the computer, but the rigidity of their syntax restricts their use to trained programmers. This has served to keep computing in a 'closed shop' environment and retain for it the image of a mystical art.

With the advent of the inexpensive micro, however, the closed shop was breached and it became obvious that, if the full potential of the micro as a tool was to be realized, software had to be developed which made it available to non-experts – such as managers. Packages such as Spreadsheets and Database Query Languages began to appear and, as they proliferated, they acquired the generic title of Fourth Generation Languages (4GLs).

4GLs are not languages in the same sense as third generation HLLs. The latter were procedural (the programmer had to define the procedure, step by step, for achieving a result) and general purpose (they could be used to solve a wide range of problems). A 4GL, on the other hand, is non-procedural (it tells the computer what to do rather than how to do it) and is usually restricted to a specific function, often existing only to facilitate the use of a single software product, such as a proprietary spreadsheet, database or report generator. Thus 4GLs are extremely varied in their constructs and applications – unlike the first three generations of languages, each of which has a typical form.

Perhaps the most important aspect of a 4GL is that it is **user friendly**. This implies that users do not have to learn a complicated non-English syntax in order to use the language. Thus, a statement such as LIST ALL PERSONNEL IN THE COMPANY WITH A DEGREE IN MATHEMATICS AND

MORE THAN FIVE YEARS EXPERIENCE may be acceptable as a 4GL command. The software within the computer translates this into all the actions necessary for achieving the desired result. In addition, there is often a 'help' facility which provides the user with prompts of what is acceptable as input at any given stage in the development of the user's application. Further, there are languages based on menus on the screen, which reduce the user's input to a minimum.

In general, 4GLs are interactive – that is, they guide the user into making an input on the screen and then respond to it. Error checking is thus immediate (on-line) and this saves time over the compilation methods of third generation HLLs. To guide users, many 4GLs use screen formats such that making inputs is like filling in a form. Screen aids such as the mouse and joystick are frequently used for 4GL input to graphics packages. In order to achieve dialogue between user and computer, 4GLs are usually not compiled, but are translated into machine language by an **interpreter**. This translates instruction by instruction, giving appropriate results at each step, and does not normally store a complete object program. The number of object instructions generated from each source instruction is an order of magnitude higher than for a third generation HLL, i.e. between twenty and eighty. The use of a 4GL, therefore, demands far greater computer resources (power and storage) than former languages, but hardware technology has provided these resources, in recent computers, cheaply and in miniature.

SUMMARY

A computer's electronic logic is composed of two-state, or binary, devices. These restrict computers to functioning in binary patterns, and the codes created by manufacturers for the operation of their computers are called machine languages. These form the lowest level of computer language.

Programmers, however, avoid the problems of working in machine language by writing their programs in assembly or high level languages. Assembly languages are written in a mnemonic, or memory-jogging, code and their instructions are translated into machine language instructions on a one-to-one ratio by a program called an assembler. Assembly languages, being low level, force the programmer to know how his instructions and data are handled within the computer, so good programmers can achieve high efficiency in the use of both storage and the CPU.

Third generation HLLs are still further removed from the operations within the machine. They are closer to normal language and allow programmers with a knowledge only of the language but not of the computer to write effective programs. Their efficiencies are seen as programmer rather than run-time efficiencies: they allow programs to be written quickly and readily understood, modified and corrected (or **debugged**). HLLs are translated into the machine language of the computer in use by programs known as compilers.

Fourth generation languages provide a user friendliness

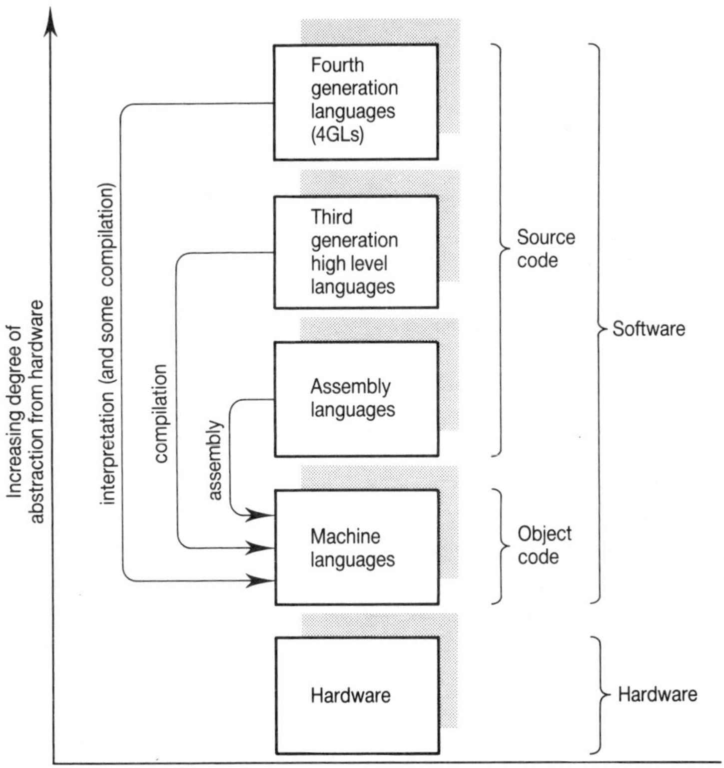

Figure 10.1 *Levels of computer language.*

which permits non-programmers to work directly with computers. They provide interactive dialogue with users and employ a number of aids, such as screen formats and menus, to ensure that users do not need to learn complex languages. Thus they put the computer, as a tool, more directly into the hands of those who need to use it.

The levels of computer languages are seen in Figure 10.1. Each level provides the programmer with a greater degree of abstraction from the **hardware.** The figure also distinguishes software from hardware and defines the methods of translation from higher levels of language to machine language.

CHAPTER 11

OPERATING SYSTEMS

System software consists of those programs which are supplied as part of the computer system and which contribute to its basic functioning. Assemblers and compilers, which were discussed in the previous chapter, are examples of essential elements of system software. Equally fundamental to computer operation are **operating systems.** They form an interface between the computer hardware and users' applications programs, and provide and control a number of facilities which improve computing efficiency. Indeed, without them, computing would be merely rudimentary.

As well as being isolated from the manipulation of instructions and data within the computer, the programmer wishes to be independent of the way in which the computer handles its internal **housekeeping**, i.e. he wishes to input his program to the computer without concerning himself with where it is stored or how it is scheduled to run. He also wishes to initiate the input or output of information with a simple command in the language he is using, without having to know the details of how the computer communicates with the input/output (I/O) peripheral devices. However, the detailed instructions for the execution of such functions must exist within the computer's store, so that they can be called to execute the required functions when necessary – in response either to the needs of a user's application program or to the internal housekeeping requirements of the computer itself. These instructions are embodied in a series of programs which together comprise the operating system. An operating system is designed to optimize the **throughput** of the computer. Figure 11.1 provides a schematic diagram of some of its typical functions, and descriptions of these are given below.

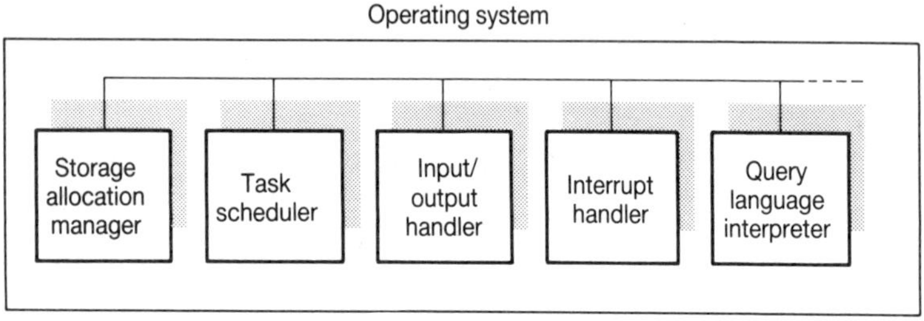

Figure 11.1 *Examples of programs included in an operating system.*

THE ESSENTIAL OPERATING SYSTEM FUNCTIONS

One of the main duties of the operating system is **storage management**. When a new program or data is input to a computer, an area of memory consisting of the appropriate number of locations needs to be allocated for its storage. Since more than one program may be held in memory at any one time, the operating system must maintain a record of where each is stored so that it does not allocate new programs or data to memory already in use. This record also allows programs and data to be accessed and recalled for use at run-time. Further, storage must periodically be rationalized; then the space occupied by obsolete information is made available for re-use. Storage management is thus a complex task and is a prime function of an operating system.

The electronic central processing unit (CPU), within which all instructions are processed, is exceedingly fast by comparison with I/O devices. If it had to idle for all periods during which I/O was in progress, the computer's efficiency would be unacceptably, and indeed uneconomically, low. The operating system therefore arranges for the CPU to be employed on other tasks while I/O is in progress. These tasks may derive from a single program or from interleaving a number of programs. The technique of optimizing CPU use by **scheduling** the different tasks or programs is known as **timesharing**.

These features of an operating system allow what is known as **batch processing**, which is usually carried out on a mainframe computer. In this manner of working, the computer operator inputs a number of jobs at a time into the machine, and it is the operating system which allocates storage and schedules the running of the programs, timesharing them as appropriate. Programs written for scientific purposes generally require less I/O than commercial jobs. Indeed some mathematical programs may take a long time to run and not provide any output until their completion. They do not therefore relinquish the processor to allow timesharing and are said to be **processor bound.**

For batch processing, the operating system is designed to **interrupt** such programs after set times so as to allow timesharing and give other programs a chance to be run. By contrast, jobs which occupy I/O devices for prolonged periods are said to be **I/O bound**. Batch processing is a usual means of operation at **computer centres**, such as at the commercial computing departments of large firms, where very large numbers of jobs are handled daily.

Timesharing also applies to the scheduling of users on terminals where rapid response gives each the impression of exclusive CPU attention. Indeed it was only the development of sophisticated operating systems which allowed these **multi-user** systems to be introduced. Clearly their efficient operation requires the CPU to be informed of progress on peripheral equipment – e.g. a printing or reading device has finished a job or a terminal user has typed in a command. Signals designed to convey such information, which would cause the CPU to suspend the current job and attend to another, are known as interrupts. It is an important duty of the operating system to handle these interrupts in an order determined by preprogrammed priorities.

The operating system also contains the program which controls communication with the computer's terminals, i.e. **on-line** users. These users require more than an ordinary high level language can offer since they also need to attract the computer's attention, identify themselves so as to gain acceptance to a secure system, etc. Languages which provide such facilities are known as **man/machine languages** (MMLs). They provide an interface, between the user and the machine, known as the **man/machine interface** (MMI). MML commands are translated by an interpreter which is usually a part of the operating system. This interprets the source commands, instruction by instruction, at run-time, so interpretation is a lengthy process, although it may be adequately fast compared with the time to input commands at a terminal. It should be noted that interpreters are not peculiar to man/machine languages. The popular high level language, BASIC, has traditionally been interpreted and its interpreter has not been a part of the operating system, but a separate item of system software. Only quite recently have BASIC compilers been developed. As was seen in the previous chapter, interpreters provide the usual means of translating fourth generation languages.

The examples given above illustrate the main functions performed by general purpose operating systems, although there are many others which may be required for other purposes. For instance, computers which form part of duplicated or multiprocessor systems need operating systems to handle duplicated secondary storage devices and to communicate with the other computers in the system. Further, computers which send data to other distant computers need programs which provide and recognize the **transmission**

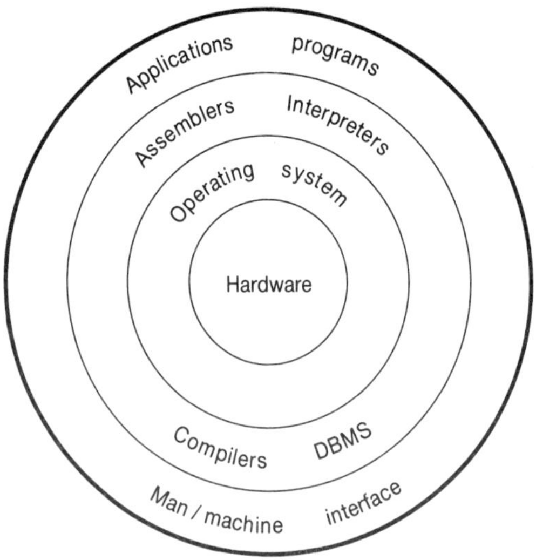

Figure 11.2 *Functional levels of a computer system.*

protocols, and these may be provided as part of an operating system.

An operating system of some sort is thus indispensable to all but the most rudimentary of computer applications. It is a necessary part of the computer system and is permanently available to make the hardware do more than mere processing. At the same time it greatly increases the efficiency of the programmer.

With an operating system, the computer system can be perceived as a collection of interacting hardware and software elements, functioning at different levels (see Figure 11.2). The lowest of these is the CPU with its associated arithmetic and logic functions. The next, being the software which interacts directly with the hardware, is the operating system. The third level consists of compilers, assemblers, interpreters and database management systems (DBMSs), all of which offer direct services to applications programs and on-line users. The final level comprises the applications programs and man/machine interfaces themselves.

CHAPTER 12

DATABASES

Any organization requires information (data) for its operations and existence. It functions best when its data is up-to-date, easily accessible and consistent across the organization. In traditional methods of storing information, each user of the data has maintained his own files independently of other users. Thus, much of the data is stored two or more times and, since each file holder is responsible for updating his own files, lack of knowledge of changes leads to out-of-date information being held, and inconsistency of data across the organization.

A user's conception of data usually takes a tabular form. This is illustrated in Figure 12.1 where a limited range of the data required by three departments in a company – the administrative, operational and payroll departments – is depicted. Considering the sum of all this data, there is a great deal of redundancy and a consequent difficulty in maintaining correctness and consistency.

Even when computers became a widespread tool for the storage and maintenance of information, departments tended to retain their files on their own machines, so perpetuating the problems of paper-based systems. Then developments in software resulted in the database management system (DBMS), which is a package of software designed to formalize the storage and access of data so as to overcome these problems.

DATABASE SYSTEMS

A database system can be said to comprise four constituents: hardware, data, software and users.

The *hardware* consists of the storage media on which the

Administrative department's file

Name	Date of birth	Home address	Department
BROWN, J S	17.9.33	16 SINFIELD ST, READING, BERKS, RG17 9XF	OP
SMITH, A T B	4.6.47	39 WELLARD RD, LONDON, N29 4RP	OP

Operational department's file

Name	Duty	Normal hours this week	Overtime hours this week
BROWN, J S	LATHE	37	6
SMITH, A T B	FITTER	37	2

Payroll department's file

Name	Department	Basic rate of pay	O/T rate of pay	Normal hours this week	Overtime hours this week	Basic pay	O/T pay	Total pay
BROWN, J S	OP	6.85	8.56	37	6	253.45	51.36	304.81
SMITH, A T B	OP	5.85	7.30	37	2	216.45	14.60	231.05

Figure 12.1 *Typical user's views of data (tabular), represented by the files (simplified) of three company departments.*

data is held. In a few cases this may be RAM, but usually RAM is inadequate so secondary storage, in the form of disks, is necessary.

The *data* is the contents of the database itself which, defined simply, is a computerized filing system.

The *users* may be terminal users requiring access to the database, or application programs, resident in the computer, which must access the database in order to carry out their functions.

The *software* consists of a DBMS which performs a number of functions. First it defines the structure into which the data must be loaded when the database is being created.

This allows the database designers to define the relationships between the types of data in the database, while adhering to the structure imposed by the DBMS. Then it provides the means of accessing the data in the database – for inserting new data, updating information already there, or retrieving stored data to apply it to some use. In doing this, it allocates the data to carefully chosen files in storage and creates links between files which provide paths for accessing the data. The software also contains algorithms for accessing the data. These algorithms are activated by users' commands which define the data to be accessed. These commands usually form a **query language** and are of a high level, such as 'Display all employees in Department X', or 'Display the department in which Smith, A T B works'. The DBMS interprets the commands of the query language into instructions suitable for activating the processor to carry out the necessary tasks.

An overview of a database system, showing these four components, is illustrated in Figure 12.2. The DBMS is seen to form a layer round the database itself. In doing this, it provides the users with a level of abstraction from the database. They do not need to know its structure or how one item of data is stored relative to another. They only need to know the

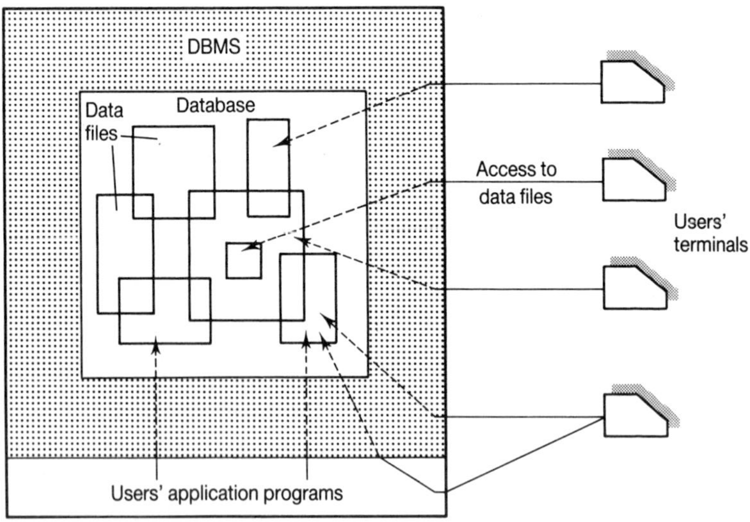

Figure 12.2 *Overview of a database system.*

commands which achieve their desired results. At the same time, the DBMS provides a layer of protection for the data in the database. Since it only accesses the data according to pre-programmed methods, it protects the data against accidental (or even malicious) actions of users.

ADVANTAGES OF DATABASE SYSTEMS

Figure 12.2 shows that different users require to access different files within a database and that the information within those files overlaps. Judicious use of storage techniques can therefore minimize multiple appearances of data items within the database. However, total avoidance of redundancy, though often possible, usually adds complexity to the means of storage and access and may therefore be imprudent. Nevertheless, a database system does provide central control of the database. Since the DBMS defines the structure of the database, it maintains a record of all appearances of each data item and its relationship to other items. Thus, when any item is updated (or deleted) all necessary actions are automatically carried out to maintain the integrity of the whole database.

Maintenance of integrity is also assisted by the ability to impose restrictions of access on users. This is achieved by the use of passcards to gain the use of a terminal, recognition by the system of which terminal access is being made from, and the use of passwords to gain access to various functions within the system. By this, access to any data can be restricted to authorized users of that data and updating can be further restricted to certain nominated users. Thus, changes in address may be restricted to the administrative department, changes in pay to the payroll department, and changes in duty to an operational department, while all these changes are made for the benefit of all users.

By ensuring that only the correct users update information, not only is security of the data achieved, but the application of standards to the storage, representation and validation of data is facilitated. With responsibility so easily defined, the will to employ standards is usually enhanced.

Finally, although redundancy is seldom eliminated altogether, database systems make the sharing of data a natural occurrence. They encourage designers of new applications to check whether the data they require is already in storage before choosing to expand the database for their data.

Storage of Data

However data is represented on paper, within the computer it is stored in memory locations. These, as described in Chapter 8, are words of storage composed of memory elements, or bits.

The smallest entity of data stored within a computer is a **field.** The size of a field depends on the size of the data entity being stored. It need not be an integer number of words and may only consist of a single bit.

A **record** is a collection of data items or fields. The items are normally related so that their amalgamation creates a meaningful unit. Figure 12.3 shows a record corresponding to the administrative department's information requirements in Figure 12.1. The four fields are seen to occupy a total of six words.

A **file** is a collection of records. For example, if the administrative department held one record for every employee, its employee file would consist of all these records.

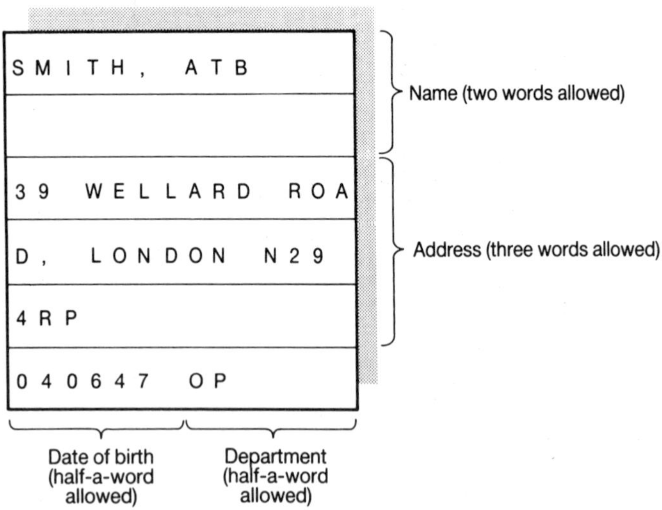

Figure 12.3 *Data record consisting of four fields and six words.*

1	2	3	4	5	6	7	8	9	10	11	12
Name	Date of birth	Home address	Dept.	Duty	Basic rate of pay	O/T rate of pay	Normal hours this week	O/T hours this week	Basic pay	O/T pay	Total pay
BROWN, J S	17.9.33	16 SINFIELD ST, READING, BERKS, RG17 9XF	OP	LATHE	6.85	8.56	37	6	253.45	51.36	304.81
SMITH, A T B	4.6.47	39 WELLARD RD, LONDON, N29 4RP	OP	FITTER	5.85	7.30	37	2	216.45	14.60	231.05

Figure 12.4 *Conceptual view of the data required by the three departments as shown in Figure 12.1.*

Given that three departments want their information presented to them in the form shown in the three tables of Figure 12.1, does the data have to be stored within the database in the same way? No, there are many ways in which the data can be structured. It is the DBMS which, having extracted the various items of data from the database, assembles them into the form suitable to the particular user.

A conceptual view of the database appropriate to the data of Figure 12.1 is shown in Figure 12.4. From this view, the table for the administrative department would be assembled from columns 1, 2, 3 and 4. The operational department's table comes from columns 1, 3, 5, 8 and 9. The table for the payroll department comes from columns 1, 4, 6, 7, 8, 9, 10, 11 and 12. This view of the database avoids duplication of data, though this is not necessarily the case in practice.

There are three main forms of database. These are the **network**, the **hierarchical** and the **relational**, each named after the manner in which the data within it is structured.

The network database allows any item of data to be connected to any number of other items. 'Connections' are in software and are not physical, but they form a notional network which can become extremely complex. This results in network databases being very large and difficult to maintain. Indeed, they are not widely used and their applications are limited to mainframe computers.

A hierarchical database is very efficient for data which naturally falls into a hierarchy, such as the contents of a telephone directory or an employee register. Even then, it is only efficient if searches for data start at the top and work down. Complexity sets in if a search starts at the bottom and has to work up the hierarchy.

The relational database is based on a tabular structure – similar to the conceptual model of Figure 12.4. Items of data with chosen relationships to each other are stored in tables, or **relations**, and software links are created to connect related tables. The problem of having to traverse hierarchically structured links are overcome – though at the cost of size.

Early databases were hierarchical, but now relational databases are more effective and more popular, in spite of their requirement for more computer resources. All databases require significant computer resources for their satisfactory application and the largest can only be implemented on mainframes. However, there are versions of both hierarchical and relational databases designed for use on micros.

DISTRIBUTED DATABASES

Using local area networks (LANs), or even wide area networks (WANs), database principles can be extended to cover data which is stored in a number of computers. Then each computer can store the data which is most frequently accessed by its users and it can access the data on any of the other computers when required. This provides users in, perhaps, widely separated locations, with apparently immediate access to vast volumes of data, while local storage and the use of the communications network are optimized.

The computers need not be widely separated. For instance, each department within a company may maintain its own computer for the storage of locally important data, while having access to other company files held on other machines – perhaps within the same building.

In one respect, a distributed system can be said to comprise a number of databases. However, they are not disparate. A significant and important principle is that the user is unaware that any of the data is not stored locally. The same simple commands bring data from any part of the network and this gives the impression of a single database. For this to be so there clearly needs to be a considerable degree of logic in the controlling software and this adds complexity to the DBMS.

As was mentioned in Chapter 3, implementing such networks is not trivial and distributed databases are not yet at the stage where they can be taken for granted. Nevertheless, they exist and should become more prominent as the software which controls them is improved in efficiency and reliability.

CHAPTER 13

WHAT MAKES THE COMPUTER WORK

A computer is a software-based machine, which is to say, its actions are determined by the programs of instructions stored in its own memory. However, although the software provides the schedule for what is to be done, it is the hardware which carries out the actions. The computer's electronic logic circuitry provides the capability of performing a limited number of very basic functions. These form the computer's **instruction set** and are the building blocks of all tasks carried out by the machine.

Before a task can be computerized, its method of execution, or **algorithm**, must be clearly defined. This is then translated into a program to be executed by the computer, each program instruction depending on the basic functions of the computer for its processing. Clearly, the software must only instruct the computer to perform those functions for which it is wired, otherwise the instructions could not be understood or executed by the machine.

This chapter discusses the means by which a computer is able to carry out processing. Although this is ultimately done within the hardware instruction set, it is the result of the software instructions, so it is as well first to understand how software exists within a computer and how it interacts with the hardware.

WHAT IS SOFTWARE?

It has been seen that a memory element is a hardware device which can exist in one of two states. When it is in one state it represents a binary '1' and, when in the other, a binary '0'. A computer word consists of a number of such elements wired so as to form an entity. The storage of a word of software is therefore the setting of the elements of a word in memory to represent a specified pattern of binary bits.

To use the analogy of a memory element being like an electric switch, we could consider the switch to represent a '1' when it is ON and a '0' when it is OFF. Or imagine a tiny electronic see-saw which represents a '1' when it slopes in one direction and a '0' when it slopes in the other. The point is illustrated in Figure 13.1 where an 8-bit word, written in binary digits, is shown with the symbolic representations of the see-saw and switch.

Software within a computer is thus seen to have no existence independent of the hardware. Should the question be asked 'How does the software interact with and therefore influence the hardware?', the answer is that, in this context, the software *is* the hardware. It is simply the *result* of hardware elements being set in a particular configuration.

Within the memory, all software is stored in the same way: instructions, addresses, and data are all stored together as strings of bits. Only by their relative sequential positions in a program are they distinguishable from each other. When processing is to be carried out, a program instruction is transferred to the control unit and its bit pattern interpreted by the unit's logic circuitry. In this way it is determined which elements of the machine's instruction set must be employed in order for the instruction to be obeyed. This is the beginning of **processing** which will be discussed in the next chapter.

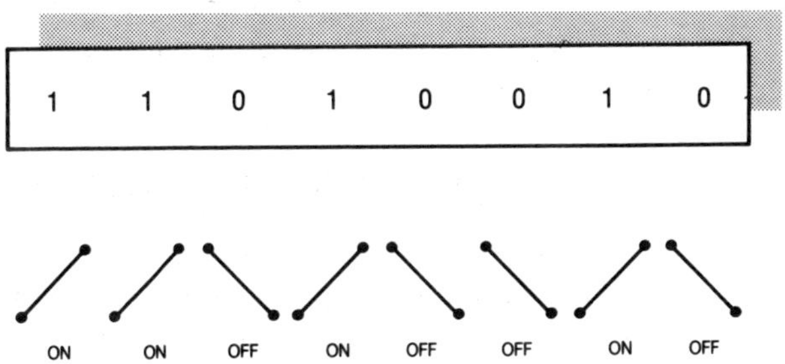

Figure 13.1 *A software word, in binary notation, with see-saw and switch analogies.*

THE INSTRUCTION SET

The hardware of every computer is designed to perform a number of basic functions. These include arithmetic functions, such as addition and subtraction; and logical functions such as AND and OR. Since the activity of a computer actually takes place in the hardware (although it is determined by the software), every task that the computer performs must be composed of one or more of these functions. They are wired into the hardware of the machine and they make up the computer's instruction set. Figure 13.2, an update of Figure 10.1 which showed the levels of computer language (p. 93), shows that the hardware with which the machine language interacts is the instruction set.

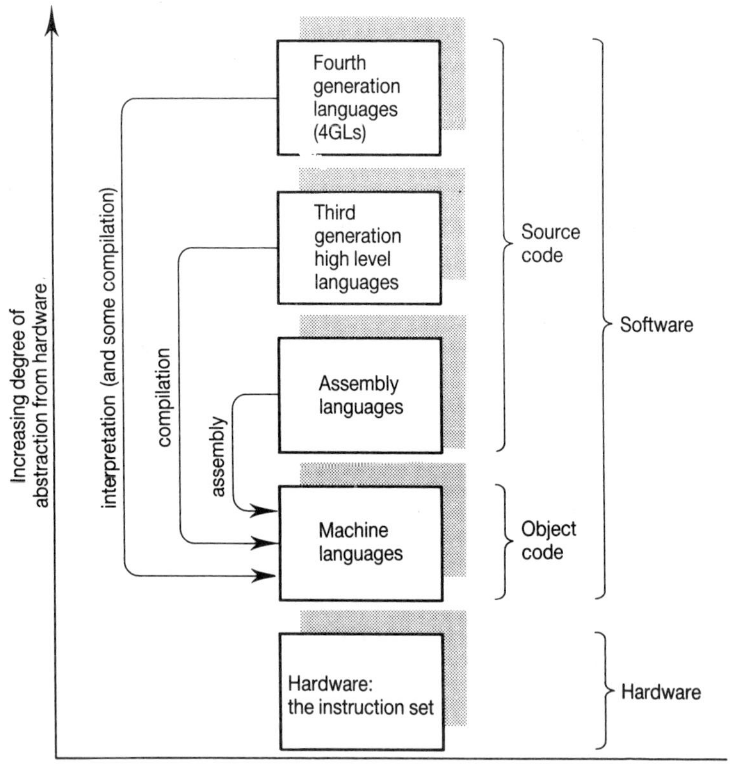

Figure 13.2 *Machine language employs the computer's instruction set.*

Every model of computer has its own instruction set, which is a critical aspect of the machine's design. Since every additional computer function adds to the circuitry of the machine, it also adds to the cost. A computer with an extensive instruction set is therefore likely to be more expensive than one whose instruction set is limited. However, until recently, it would almost certainly have been faster, since a larger number of actions could be executed at high speed in the electronic hardware. In choosing a computer, therefore, there was a trade-off between cost and speed.

The development which has superseded this is that of the **reduced instruction set computer** (RISC). Studies have shown that a minority of the instruction set functions were employed for a vast majority of the processing time. Manufacturers, therefore, have been able to reduce hardware costs by developing computers with smaller (or reduced) instruction sets, without significant effect on the capabilities of the machines.

If a computer is to possess the flexibility for which it is renowned, its instruction set must contain those functions which are the most elementary in arithmetic and logic processes. Then all other, more complex, functions can be executed using the elementary functions as building blocks. It is often an asset to have additional, more complex functions in the instruction set, but the fundamental functions must be present. If a machine can only perform complex (or relatively complex) functions, then it is more specific to a certain type of application. It will be efficient in performing that application, but less able to perform others, particularly those which require the missing elementary functions. Such a computer would not be general-purpose.

To illustrate this point, consider the functions of addition and multiplication. Addition is the most basic arithmetic function, and evey computer is expected to possess the circuitry to add two numbers in a single electronic operation. Multiplication is also a very frequently used arithmetic operation and is therefore a useful inclusion in the circuitry within the instruction set. However, although it is usual, it is not essential, since multiplication is not a basic operation: it can be achieved by using the addition function. For example, 27 multiplied by five can be resolved in a single operation of multiplication, but it can also be achieved by starting with a value of zero and adding 27 to it five times. Similarly, division can be achieved by successive subtraction.

Each execution of a basic function is referred to as an **execute cycle**. The time of an execute cycle varies according to the speed of the computer, but is generally measured in nanoseconds (ns). Clearly, multiplication is performed far more quickly if it is provided as a basic function, and occupies a single execute cycle, than if it requires a number (perhaps a very large number) of execute cycles in the application of successive additions.

A computer must have the capability of carrying out any function which is called for by a programmer in his program – or the program could not be executed. Thus, any necessary function not provided within the computer's instruction set must be achieved by software making use of those functions which do exist in the instruction set. It has already been shown that elementary functions, provided in the instruction set, can be used as building blocks for more complex functions. The way to achieve this is by having a software program to utilize the elementary functions in the appropriate way. Considering the example of multiplication of 27 by five by successive

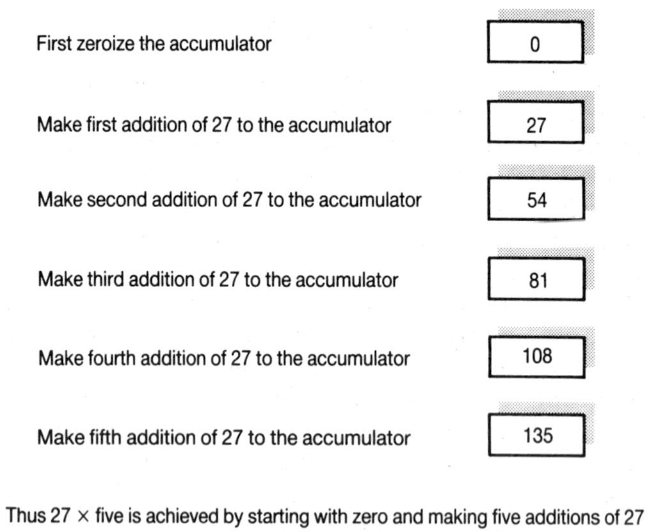

Figure 13.3 *Example of multiplication by successive addition.*

additions, as illustrated in Figure 13.3, a section of program to achieve this (written in an understandable form, and not in any computer language) would be:

```
ZEROIZE THE ACCUMULATOR
ZEROIZE Z
WHILE Z LESS THAN 5
        ADD 27 TO ACCUMULATOR
        ADD 1 TO Z
(Z is a counter to ensure the correct number of additions)
```

The above section of program would leave the result of 27 multiplied by five in the accumulator. The next part of the program (not shown here) would provide the instructions for how the result is to be used.

If a computer's instruction set does not possess the capability of executing a particular function (say, multiplication) then the necessary software may be written by an **applications programmer.** Alternatively, it may be acquired from a library of precompiled routines, kept for the purpose. More usually, however, it is provided as a **macro** by the computer manufacturer.

MACROS

Computer manufacturers supplement their instruction sets by providing, with their computers, software to carry out frequently needed functions not included within the instruction sets. This software takes the form of special subroutines called macros which are permanently stored in binary form, in read-only memory (ROM), or at least in memory which is protected against access by applications programs.

As far as an applications programmer is concerned, the functions are simply provided within the machine and he is unaware that they are not within the instruction set. They therefore offer a convenience to the programmer, though they do not provide the speed of performing their operations which circuitry in the hardware would have done. Figure 13.4 shows how macros add a level of abstraction between the computer's instruction set and its machine language.

In use, a macro is inserted into an application program like a subroutine when the compiler translates the program into

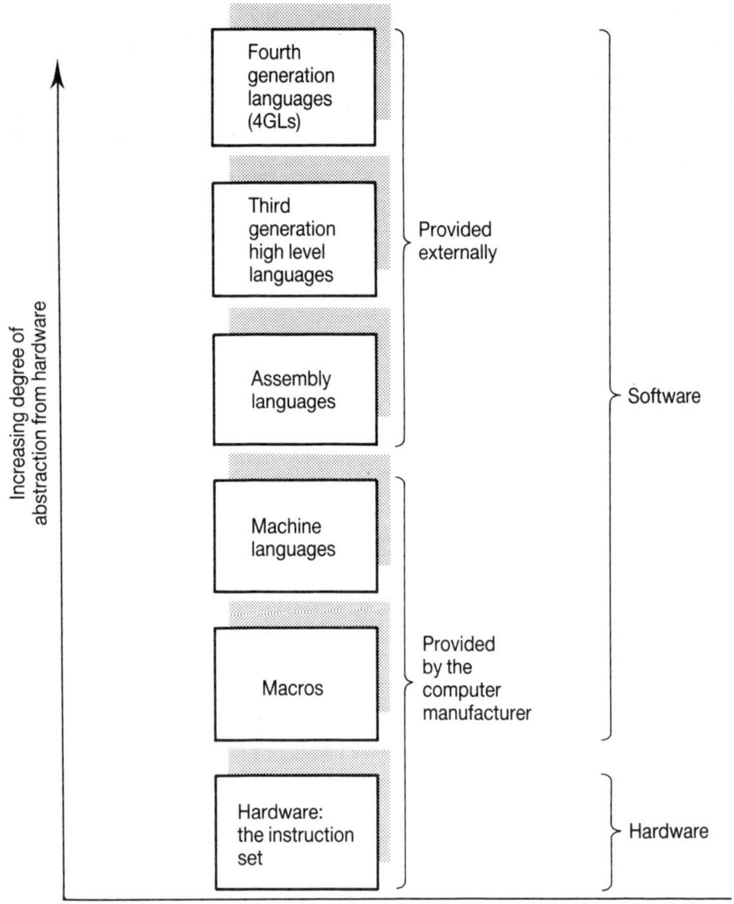

Figure 13.4 *Macros add a level of abstraction between a computer's instruction set and its machine language.*

machine language. If the function required by the program instruction (say addition or multiplication) is within the instruction set, the compiler simply translates the program instruction into its machine language equivalent which will activate the function at run-time.

When the function is provided within the computer in the form of a macro, a translation of the instruction into binary form could not exist as a single instruction. The compiler, therefore, replaces the original programming language instruction with the macro in the machine code (binary) version of the application program. Then, at run-time, the instructions provided by the macro are executed as part of the program, and the process is transparent to the ordinary computer user.

CHAPTER 14
PROCESSING

Having discussed first hardware and then software in the previous chapters, it is now possible to describe the way in which the two interact to carry out **processing**. The basis of this was described in the previous chapter. This chapter contains descriptions, first in general terms and then in more detail, of how a computer executes the instructions contained within a program and how it handles the program's data.

As was seen in the previous chapter, the hardware functions of a computer are entirely basic and their number is limited. Carrying out a task therefore consists of huge numbers of repetitions of the same simple hardware actions, as dictated by the software. This is one source of the computer's flexibility. If the actions of which a machine is capable become more complex at the expense of basic functions, the machine becomes more specialized in its application and less general-purpose. The design principle of using software stored in the computer's own memory to control basic hardware functions and thus produce a general-purpose processing system is attributed to John von Neumann, the American mathematician.

THE VON NEUMANN MODEL

In 1946 a group of engineers and mathematicians led by John von Neumann proposed the design and method of working which has, until recently, remained the model for all digital computers. The design is of a system composed of hardware and software. The processing hardware consists of only two essential components: a processor which interprets and executes instructions and a memory in which the instructions are stored (see Figure 14.1). The software, in the form of binary code only, is made up of the programs of instructions and their associated data. The system's operation is dependent only on the software contained in the memory and is not constrained by the hardware. The hardware's operation is elementary and is based entirely on two functions of the processor. The first is its ability to access any memory location and alter or retrieve its contents. The second is processing which is performing certain functions, using the processor's own electronic logic circuitry.

Another significant point is that a processor is a **single thread** device. It follows a single path through a program, executing sequentially one instruction at a time. Further, the path is defined within the program itself; it is a logical one and

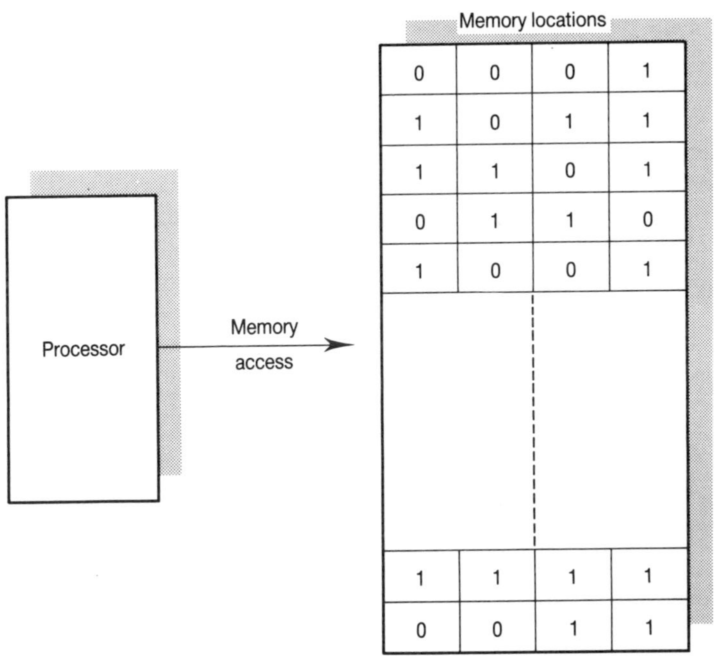

Figure 14.1 *von Neumann computer design in which the hardware consists of only two elements: a processor and a memory. The processor can access any memory location.*

not merely dependent on the order in which the instructions appear. Thus the order in which the program's instructions are executed can be made to be conditional on circumstances that arise from the data as the program is being executed. This principle of conditional branching was seen in the discussion of high level language on p. 90.

In the normal course of operation, the processor retrieves a program instruction from memory and then **executes** it. Execution takes the form of interpreting the instruction within the processor's logical circuitry and then obeying it, i.e. carrying out the operations designated by the instruction. These usually include the altering or retrieval of the contents of other memory locations, and the operation on retrieved data by functions in the hardware's instruction set. When all the operations required by an instruction have been completed, the processor retrieves the contents from the next location in the logical path being followed and, because of its position in the logical path, expects it to be an instruction. In this way the next cycle commences.

The data being manipulated is stored in binary form, as are the instructions, and the processor can only distinguish between them by the order in which they are presented to its circuitry. This will become clear as the manner of processing a program is described in the following example.

EXECUTING A PROGRAM

When a program is input to the computer, the operating system allocates it to free memory and stores the address of the program's first instruction in a special register, known as the address register, from which it is retrieved at run-time. The addresses of the data locations are stored within the program itself, as though they were a part of it, so that the data is correctly accessed at the appropriate place within the program.

Figure 14.2a shows a plan of 16 consecutive locations of storage in which a simple program and its data are stored. The program is for adding two numbers together. The instructions are not in any computer language, but are written so that their interpretations may be clear to the reader. Typical binary translations of the contents of the locations in Figure 14.2a are depicted in Figure 14.2b and these will be discussed later.

Location number	(a)	(b)			
0					
1	Zeroize accumulator	0	0	0	1
2	Add to accumulator the contents of the location whose address is in the next location	1	0	1	1
3	11	1	0	1	1
4	Add to accumulator the contents of the location whose address is in the next location	1	0	1	1
5	12	1	1	0	0
6	Write contents of accumulator to the location whose address is in the next location	1	0	0	1
7	13	1	1	0	1
8					
9					
10					
11	11	1	0	1	1
12	4	0	1	0	0
13	15	1	1	1	1
14					
15					

Figure 14.2 *Storage of a program and its data (a) in descriptive form and (b) in binary form.*

Now, to show how a computer executes software instructions, the processing of the program in Figure 14.2a will be followed.

When the program is about to be run, the control unit retrieves the instruction from the address stored in the address register. This is the first in the program and is an instruction to zeroize the accumulator. This is a precaution against corruption of the present operation by the results of previous calculations. It is not necessary to write such an instruction when programming in a high level language, for it is inserted by the compiler when the latter translates the program into machine language. However, it is often necessary in an assembly language program. This means that an assembly language programmer needs to know more about what goes on within the computer, which makes learning an assembly language useful training for a programmer.

When the control unit has instructed the ALU to zeroize the accumulator, the value in the address register is incremented. The new value is the address of the next instruction in the program and this is retrieved. It is an ADD instruction and there is therefore a need for both an item of data and the address of that data. The instruction itself says where the address of the data is stored – in the next location (location 3) – so the control unit retrieves the contents of location 3, which consist of the number 11. It therefore knows that the data to be added to the accumulator is in location 11. It sends out the necessary electrical signals, to the memory and the ALU for the contents of location 11 to be transferred to the ALU and added to the accumulator. The value of the accumulator (its contents) then changes from 0 to 11.

Having done all that was necessary to execute the previous instruction (i.e. having completed the **machine cycle**), the control unit moves sequentially downwards through the program by incrementation of the address register, expecting to find an instruction (rather than, say, an address) in location 4. It therefore retrieves the contents of location 4 and proceeds to interpret it as an instruction. This is a repeat of the previous instruction, and the control unit retrieves the contents of location 5 to find the address of the required data. The value of the contents of location 5 is 12, so the data required must be stored in location 12. The control unit then dispatches the signals for the contents of location 12 to be sent to the ALU and added to the accumulator. The value of the contents of the accumulator thus increases by four, from 11 to 15.

Another machine cycle is thus completed and the control unit then seeks the next instruction in location 6 and, as a result of it, arranges for the contents of the accumulator (15) to be transferred to location 13.

Any practical computer has a memory of more than 16 locations, and the above is a very simplified example, but it serves to demonstrate the method of processing within a computer. It also shows that at the machine level nothing can be taken for granted. Every action to be performed must be catered for in the software. Also, since the hardware is only capable of the very basic actions for which it is wired, program instructions need to break down every task into those basic actions which make up the computer's instruction set.

THE BINARY FORM

Having discussed generally the manner in which processing is carried out, it is appropriate to use the binary form of the software to illustrate the logic of the computer. The example program's simple addition may be expressed in a high level language as a single statement, such as:

$$C = A + B$$

To translate this into machine code, the compiler is first required to allocate locations, with known addresses, to the variables *A*, *B* and *C*. Then the instruction is translated by the compiler into machine language as shown in Figure 14.2b, the interpretations of the contents of the various locations being as in the corresponding locations in Figure 14.2a and the earlier description. Figure 14.2b is extremely simplified since it only uses 4-bit words. A practical computer would have at least an 8-bit word, but the example illustrates the principle.

Likewise, an assembly language version of a similar program was shown on p. 88:

```
CLA    / Zeroize (or clear) accumulator
ADD A/ Add contents of address A to accumulator
ADD B/ Add contents of address B to accumulator
STO C / Store contents of accumulator in address C
```

This is translated by an assembler into the binary form already shown in Figure 14.2b.

The point has been made that program instructions and data are stored in the same form. It has also been mentioned in the earlier description of the program's execution that the processor only distinguished between instructions, addresses and data because of its sequential and logical steps through the program and not because of an intrinsic ability to recognize them. This can be seen even more clearly by considering the binary version of the program in Figure 14.2b.

When the control unit retrieves the contents of location 2, it finds the binary word '1011'. It expects this to be an *instruction* since it has completed the task given it by the previous instruction (i.e. zeroizing the accumulator). In the hypothetical machine code of this example, 1011 means 'Add to the accumulator the contents of the location whose address is in the next location'. The processor retrieves the contents of the next location and finds them to be 1011. From the interpretation of the previous instruction, it expects this to be an *address*. It therefore accesses location 1011 to find the data which it requires. The data also have the *value* 1011 (being the number 11), and the processor completes the **machine cycle** designated by the instruction by adding this value to the accumulator.

The computer has therefore had to deal with the same value (1011) in three consecutive operations and has treated it in three different ways, as an instruction, as an address and as data. In each case it has acted in accordance with a predetermined logical plan defined by the instruction and has not been influenced in its action by the value which it was handling – though of course the value influenced the results obtained. Indeed the computer has not even recognized that the three values were the same. It cannot recollect the actions which it has previously taken and is aware only of its current action. Its memory holds instructions and data which determine its future action, but does not give it a knowledge of its past.

In processing, therefore, the computer's hardware carries out a predetermined procedure to retrieve from memory a software instruction. It then acts in conformity with that instruction, before retrieving another. The hardware thus provides the means of processing while the software provides its control. Indeed, the software's control extends to determining the processing path to be taken through the program itself, thus providing computing with enormous flexibility.

PART III

TOWARDS THE FIFTH GENERATION

Recent developments, current research, and the path to fifth generation computers.

CHAPTER 15

TOWARDS THE FIFTH GENERATION

Following Japan's announcement of a ten year project which would result, in 1991, in the prototype of a fifth generation computer, the USA and Europe were obliged to announce their dedication to similar goals. Much of the research in the USA has been under the banner of the military's strategic defence initiative (SDI). In Europe, coordination has been under the Trans-Europe European Strategic Programme for Research in Information Technology (ESPRIT) and, in the UK, under the Alvey Project. These projects, however, do not consist of simple concerted efforts, but are made up of large numbers of sub-projects researching a wide variety of topics in information technology.

It was pointed out in Chapter 2 that computer hardware is now in its fourth generation, having been based on valve technology, discrete component transistors, simple integrated circuitry and, latterly, very large scale integration. Fifth generation computers, however, will not simply be a further development in hardware technology. They will be total systems, based on features provided by advances in both hardware and software. The latter includes data structures, programming techniques and, indeed, the ways of approaching the specification and solution of problems.

While there is yet no precise definition of the characteristics which will typify fifth generation systems, current thinking is that the three most likely will be **parallel processing, artificial intelligence** and free communication with users via a sophisticated **man/machine interface**. Two further areas in which advances in technology are expected to make the fifth generation superior to existing computers are developments in

software techniques and tools, and in the hardware field of even larger scale integrated circuitry – **super large scale integration** (SLSI).

Secure Computing and Parallel Processing

While parallel processing continues to be a subject of research and development, with a view to the fifth generation, it is not an altogether new field. It already exists, having arisen out of the need for secure computing.

In today's parlance, every computer application falls under the heading of information technology (IT). The range of computer uses is enormous and most of us are aware of many of them. We frequently encounter evidence of the electronic office in the form of word processors, facsimile and the facilities provided by private automatic branch exchanges – PABXs. We use or see advertised the value added services discussed in Part I. We use processor-controlled petrol pumps when we drive into service stations. We see IT in action when we book a holiday and watch the clerk interrogating a database on a remote computer.

With so much information and so many services directly dependent on computing, a computer failure can result not only in inconvenience, but also in loss of confidence, good will, livelihood and even life. Securing continuity of service is therefore essential to some applications.

Since it is not possible to guarantee that faults will not occur, security of service must be achieved by ensuring that they do not cause failure of the system. In other words, the system is designed to be fault tolerant. This implies that redundancy must be a part of the design, i.e. that the subsystems, or components of the system, must be duplicated, or replicated – according to the importance of the service.

To date, redundancy has mostly been based on the **hot stand-by** machine (see Figure 15.1), i.e. redundancy in the hardware. Whereas replacement of faulty hardware with a similar component, or module, normally results in a working system, this is in general not the case with software. The latter is not subject to wear and tear and a design or programming error in a software module will exist in all copies of that

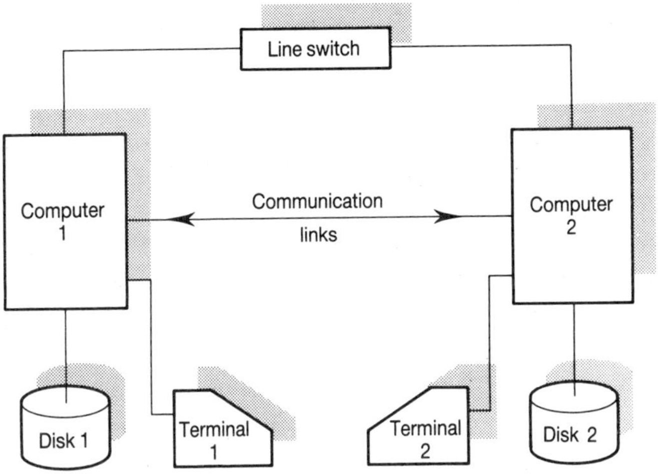

Figure 15.1 *Basic hot stand-by computer system.*

module. However, in case of corruption of software due, say, to a hardware fault or an operator's error, copies of the software in use are kept on secondary storage (usually disks) from where they can be loaded into the system if required. For these specific occurrences, software redundancy is both useful and essential.

The principle of the hot stand-by machine is that the spare computer is not switched off, but is running and in a state of readiness in case the operational machine fails. There are a number of computer **architectures** in which this principle is employed, for example, dual processing, triple processing and multi-processing, in which two, three or many computers or processors are involved. There are also a number of **modes of operation**, for example:

- **synchronous** working, in which the computers perform the same functions and compare results, using pre-programmed decision-making algorithms,
- **load sharing** in which all the processors, or computers, share the total load, with each having spare capacity as a safeguard against the failure of any one,

- the simple hot stand-by, in which the spare computer does not perform useful work while standing-by.

Clearly the implementation of any of these configurations requires a great deal more software than a single computer system. There must be:

- control software for the interworking of the machines,
- checking programs for the comparison of results and outputs,
- diagnostic software to ensure that faults are detected,
- control software to remove faulty modules from service,
- software for communication between the computers or processors.

Developments in software and testing to ensure that they perform correctly have therefore been the key factor in the provision of fault-tolerant (also referred to as **non-stop** or **resilient**) systems. With the principles of such systems established, manufacturers are now producing off-the-shelf fault-tolerant systems and these are increasingly being applied to tasks not previously associated with the need for resilience. It is likely that with further improvements in the systems, increasing miniaturization and reducing prices, fault tolerance will be an integral part of most computer systems by the next decade.

It should be noted also that provision of redundancy in a load sharing mode achieves a form of parallel processing. Whereas this is the result of different computers working together, one of the aims of fifth generation research is to employ parallel processing within a single computer. This implies the use of more than one processor within the machine, which is a departure from the von Neumann principle (see Part II) which has been the basis of computer design to date. Indeed this has already been developed in the British **transputer**, which consists of a number of microprocessors on a single chip. The system software for using these efficiently is complex, particularly as some types of applications do not gain from parallel processing as the data can only follow a single path. Inmos, the inventors of the transputer, provide a new language, OCCAM, to facilitate the development of applications programs.

As mentioned above, hardware redundancy is not proof against many software errors, nor against **common mode faults** such as power failure. Common mode failures can only be guarded against by careful planning, such as the provision of dual power supplies and independent power and transmission cables into buildings and between communicating computers.

Security against software faults is achieved in various ways. First, corruption during the transfer of data is guarded against by parity checks (as described on pp. 76–77). The chance of more widespread corruption (say, of an area of storage due to operator error or power failure) is insured against by holding duplicate copies of software on secondary storage. When these are held on disks which are an integral part of the computer system in use, they can be retrieved rapidly in the case of trouble. In addition, copies of the software on magnetic tape or removable disk may be stored off-site in case of fire or other major system catastrophe. This safeguard is advised for businesses which store their files on computer systems.

Moreover, computer systems frequently contain some applications programs which are devoted to the maintenance of the system in the event of software faults. Sometimes these programs consist only of routines which print out error messages, but more frequently they are being written to take defensive action so that the system does not fail when such faults arise.

The strongest defence against software errors is good system and program design. Modern **software engineering** methods are based on the principles of good design, thorough testing and quality assurance. Further, it is recognized that even if it were possible to write an error-free program, it would be impossible to prove that it was error-free, so software design involves not only the aim of correctness but also that of maintainability. It is unawareness of this and a lack of knowledge of how to achieve it that makes most amateur software designers and programmers a hazard in business or other consequential environments.

ARTIFICIAL INTELLIGENCE

The second main characteristic of fifth generation computers is **artificial intelligence** (AI). Early work on this involved a psychological quest for an understanding of the nature of knowledge and the processes of cognition. Projects included linguistics and translation of language in textual form. Research has also continued for many years on pattern recognition and many projects have attempted to apply this to the development of visual, auditory, speech and motor facilities for machines, i.e. robotics. However, all these phenomena depend not only on perception, but also on interpretation based on context and previous knowledge. Words carry different meanings depending on their context and, in speech, on the stress placed on them. Visually, an odd looking bit of bark on a tree is accepted as being an odd bit of bark until we learn that certain moths camouflage themselves as bits of bark. When we expect to find moths in that context we not only see them but recognize them. A baby's cry on a mountain may be assumed to be the sound of a sheep, because we do not expect to encounter a baby on a mountain.

So recognition of text, images, or sound requires not only the ability to perceive, but also a set of rules which can be applied to the interpretation of the perception – in a human these may be developed over many years of experience. One aspect of AI is therefore to discern and define these rules, and that is not easy since we are not, in general, conscious of the rules which govern the functioning of our brains. Much of our inference seems to be intuitive.

In a computer, recognition must be based on receiving an input stimulus and applying rules to it in accordance with information already stored in an information or knowledge base in the machine. In principle, this is a comparative test in which, perhaps, a huge number of comparisons are made before a match is found. The amount of data defining, say, a visual image can be considerable. The amount of processing required for the comparison of a perceived image with a number of stored images is therefore prodigious. Clearly, if a number of processors could be carrying out the comparisons in parallel, the time taken to achieve a result would be reduced substantially. Further, since many applications depend on immediate (e.g. military ballistics) or at least quick (e.g. voice input to a computer) recognition, it is essential to reduce the time taken to achieve a result. This need for faster pattern recognition has been a significant impetus behind the research into parallel processing, pattern recognition and AI.

A primitive method of seeking a comparison would be to carry out a random or sequential search of stored data. A more sophisticated method is to structure the storage of the information according to certain rules, apply tests to the input stimulus in accordance with these rules, and use the results of the tests to direct the search. Such methods, which introduce organization and strategy in attempting to reduce a search to the areas most likely to bring success, are **heuristic methods.** AI is concerned with applying heuristic methods to solving problems.

Computer systems designed to solve problems in specific fields using heuristics are known as **expert systems.** These are not necessarily concerned with pattern recognition, as discussed above, and may be designed to solve problems such as maintenance or health diagnostics.

The software for expert systems (see Figure 15.2) comprises an **inference program** (often referred to as an 'inference engine'), a **knowledge base** and a **user interface** for receipt of the problem which is input to the machine for interpretation and solution. The inference program is a logical system which uses the knowledge base to solve the current problem. The knowledge base does not contain mere data but knowledge statements, perhaps in the form of logical propositions such as:

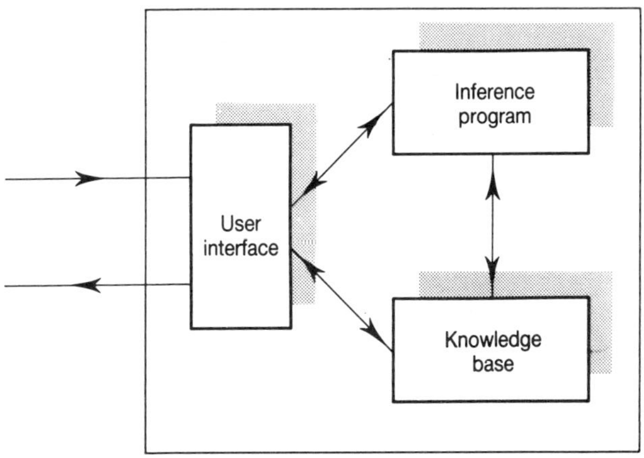

Figure 15.2 *Three main software modules of an expert system.*

IF RUNNY NOSE THEN COLD OR INFLUENZA
IF HIGH TEMPERATURE THEN INFLUENZA OR . . .
IF SORE THROAT THEN COLD OR INFLUENZA OR . . .

The knowledge base is created from information derived from human experts in the field, but it is structured so as to be easily updated and expanded to allow for new information, gained from other experts or the machine's own experience. Indeed, some machines are programmed to learn automatically from experience.

As well as the above logical propositions, or rules, there must be stored statements of fact which define the boundaries within which the rules operate. For example, a fact such as HIGH TEMPERATURE IS >37°C is an essential complement to the above rules.

As an example of how an expert system functions, consider the above IF . . . THEN statements as comprising a medical diagnostic system's knowledge base. Inputs defining the problem to be solved would take the form of symptoms:

RUNNY NOSE
or I HAVE A RUNNY NOSE
or I HAVE A SORE THROAT
or HIGH TEMPERATURE
or I HAVE A RUNNY NOSE AND A HIGH TEMPERATURE

Clearly, if the inputs to the system are to be interpreted, they must be presented in a predetermined form (such as shown above). The system is not programmed to deal with statements such as, 'I THINK I MAY HAVE A COLD'.

The inference program would then use logical processes to compare the symptom statements with the propositions in the knowledge base and thus deduce what ailment the patient is suffering from. If the input symptoms do not provide enough information for it to nominate a single disease, it may be programmed to request further information on symptoms. Without this, it would output all the possible ailments which match the given symptoms, perhaps with a probability figure for each, based on past experience.

Programming expert systems and handling knowledge bases and inference programs with efficiency is a long-winded business if ordinary high level languages are used. Languages whose syntaxes consist of propositional IF . . . THEN statements, as in the example above, are ideally suited to a quick and direct creation of knowledge bases for expert systems. Such languages are PROLOG (PROgramming in LOGic), which is favoured in Europe and Japan, LISP (LISt Programming), which is favoured in the USA, and related languages which have been based on these two.

Expert systems have already been successful in such fields as medical diagnosis and equipment fault diagnostics. However, where large knowledge bases are required, the resources necessary can be large, i.e. a very large database and a great deal of processing, leading to long response times. Nevertheless, expert systems are well suited to many areas of consultancy and their applications are extending. For example, they are sometimes integral components of larger proprietary software systems, such that the user is unaware that an expert system is present. Moreover, expert systems will be, under the title of **knowledge based systems**, integral and necessary elements of the computers of the 1990s.

SOFTWARE DEVELOPMENT

The move towards the fifth generation depends to a large extent on the development of the software elements of the systems. The importance of software in knowledge-based systems and the control of parallel processing has already been mentioned. Voice recognition and synthesis and image processing will be other applications of software technology in fifth generation systems, if the promised goal of free communication with the computers is to be achieved.

At the same time, development of all aspects of future systems is dependent on software technology. Computer aided design (discussed in Part I) has been used for some time in the design of VLSI, and it is the basis of the design of new processors and, in general, super large scale integrated circuit chips. Only by having the ease of change offered by CAD is the production and updating of circuit diagrams for chip technology a feasible task.

Moreover, the development of software itself is carried out with the use of software tools, which are themselves being developed with increasing sophistication as the need for them arises. Until the late 1960s, software development was considered an art rather than a science and designers and programmers were, in the main, left to wreak their magic. In the early 1970s software engineering was deemed to be necessary. This was intended to introduce engineering techniques and controls into the software development process so as to achieve improved and more easily amended design, more structured programs, more controlled testing and quality assurance, better documentation and hence more maintainable software with fewer errors.

Whereas even now the average designer or programmer does not adhere to good software engineering practice, formal development methods have been defined and software tools have been developed to facilitate their use. A simple example of a software tool is a compiler. This aids the programmer by allowing him to write in a high level language. Similarly, more modern tools produce design structures on a terminal's screen and prompt the designer in their use, thus ensuring that design is carried out according to a well defined method. Such a tool has the added advantage of automatically producing and storing the necessary documentation.

Beyond this, tools which are currently in vogue are the so-called fourth generation languages (4GLs). These produce program structures on the screen and prompt the programmer to complete them according to the design of the program. They then generate automatically the equivalent high level language code ready for compilation. The principle behind these is to reduce the skill and time necessary for the production of programs. They are **user friendly** in that they employ no mnemonics or obscure language and they prompt the user when help is required. The price of their use (in common with all such tools) is the need for increased computer resources – storage and time. However, with the cost of both storage and processor power considerably less than they were and still decreasing, such a price is acceptable. The reward is that human intervention can be taken a step further back from the final product. If programming does not have to be carried out manually, the code produced will exactly match the design and programming errors will not occur.

A great deal of effort is being applied to developing tools to aid the production of the specification of requirements

(SOR) and to automating the design from this. In theory, at least, this will lead to the complete automation of a software system, with its documentation, directly from the SOR. Changes to the specification will then lead to the immediate generation of an updated system. This is as yet not achieved, but it is recognized to be achievable. It is within sight and shows the direction in which software technology is advancing.

It is believed by many that this level of software automation will be a reality by the time the fifth generation systems arrive. If, at the same time, the new computers allow free communication with users, the suggestion is that there will be no need for experts in the software life cycle. This is unlikely, but software is certainly developing along an interesting and promising course.

THE FIFTH GENERATION

The phrase 'fifth generation' is now familiar in computer circles as a general indication of the direction in which computer technology is directed. As was mentioned at the beginning of this chapter, the hardware and software technologies on which a revolutionary computer system must be based are being advanced by constant research. Super large scale integrated circuitry is replacing VLSI and software engineering is producing software tools necessary for the design and development of the new machines, as well as languages of a much higher level than those currently in existence which will allow users to write programs almost in their spoken language.

Of the three characteristics which are expected to typify fifth generation computers, the first two, parallel processing and artificial intelligence, have been discussed. The hoped-for advances in man/machine interfaces, which would provide the facility of 'free communication' with users, is the third.

Free communication, in its fullest sense, implies conversation in natural language. Research is continuing into speech recognition and synthesis and already there are systems capable of outputting speech, either by synthesizing frequencies to form words or by selecting words from digitalized speech stores and assembling them to create sentences. Recognition, however, is not as far advanced. Comparing even limited categories of input sound signal against all possible interpretations requires huge volumes of storage and a great deal of processing. So far, systems can deal only with small defined vocabularies.

Whether or not there is a significant breakthrough in time for the first range of fifth generation computers, the latter are expected to provide unrestrained input/output of some form. Text recognition will be available and it is expected that the direct input of images will be too. This implies that the man/machine interface will be capable of image processing (or pattern recognition). Like voice processing, this requires enormous computer resources. The interface is therefore likely to consist of a very powerful dedicated processor (see Figure 15.3). This will receive voice, image and text input, as well as data from terminals, networks and secondary storage.

This interface processor will provide the input/output facilities for the total system. It will not only control the buffering and transport of the information, however; it will also provide processing for input and output so that the more problem-orientated processors within the system are not occupied with the considerable task of handling such complex input/output.

However the problem-orientated aspects of the system are structured, whether they are knowledge-based or data-based or involve parallel processing, the average user will be unaware of it. He will be very much aware, however, of how the

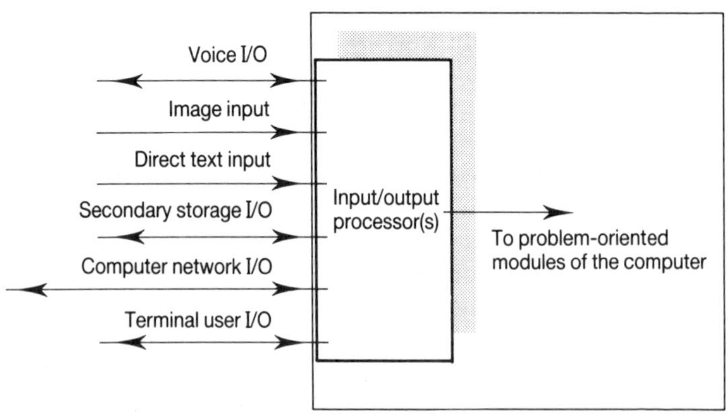

Figure 15.3 *Input/output handling will require a dedicated processor in fifth generation computers.*

man/machine interface functions and what it offers him. The ability to communicate easily with the machine and program it without having to be an expert in special languages will therefore make the fifth generation more available to users. Such availability and usefulness are goals of fifth generation research. In the main, the intention is to research, develop and introduce features not because they are feasible, but because they are seen to be useful. Fifth generation systems are therefore expected to be very powerful and very accessible. They will make computers available to tasks to which they were not hitherto applicable.

A part of this greater accessibility and applicability will be due to the use of networks (see Chapter 3). Already LANs provide computers with access to remote databases. The concept of distributed databases is on the point of becoming a reality. The full potential of fifth generation computers will only be realized when they function in integrated networks, rather than individually. For example, pattern recognition would be more rapid if its comparisons were carried out in parallel, not only on the processors of one computer, but on those of several computers. The development of software and standards for the improvement of communication between computers around the world is thus important to the effectiveness of the fifth generation.

AND BEYOND . . .

The research therefore continues. Although IT has already pervaded almost all aspects of life, even the existing technology is still a long way from being applied to its fullest. The development possibilities are not exhausted. Indeed, this chapter has only considered those areas of development which have already shown results and which are contributing directly to the fifth generation. There are many others still in their infancy but which have the potential to revolutionize computing. Worth mentioning among these is the prospect of the optical computer. For some time optical communication has been a reality, in that digital signals can be sent, at very high rates, in the form of pulses of light, over **optical fibre** cables made of fibres of extremely pure glass. However, the processing of the signals must still be carried out electrically and there need to be interfaces at the terminations of optical fibre cables to convert between the two types of signal.

Computers which handle light rather than electrical signals would not only obviate the need for such interfaces but would also operate at the speed of light, and therefore faster than current machines. They would also use less power. They would not only be immune to electrical interference, but they themselves would not create magnetic fields to interfere with other components.

As yet only very simple optical computing circuits have been demonstrated and optical computers are many years from reality. Still, there is reason to expect them eventually to replace electronic machines. Once more there will be a revolution in computing. As one technology seems to be rendering the last of its possibilities, another arrives to initiate a new cycle of research, development, and application. Information technology is capable not only of satisfying the requirements of users, but also of occupying the minds of researchers for some time to come.

GLOSSARY

Access Concerns the finding of one or more storage locations for the purpose of retrieving or altering the contents.

Access, direct The address of the target storage location is known by the computer and access is independent of the position of the target location. Disks and primary storage are directly addressable.

Access, random Access to memory such that the time to access any one location is the same as that to access any other.

Access, serial Access in which the required location can only be processed after a sequential search has been made of preceding locations, i.e. access is dependent on the relative position of the target location.

Accumulator A register, close to a computer's arithmetic logic unit, in which the results of arithmetic and logical operations are calculated. The results are transferred from the accumulator to memory pending further operations or for permanent storage.

Address A symbol, in the form of a code, name or number, which identifies a location or register in storage.

Address, direct An address which refers directly to the target location or register.

Address, indirect An address which refers to a location in which is stored the address of the target location or register.

ALGOL An acronym for ALGOrithmic Language. It is a high level language, designed to be efficient in scientific and mathematical applications. Now obsolescent.

Algorithm A procedure, or sequence of steps, for solving a problem.

AND, logical See *Logical operations.*

Applications software Software designed and written to perform specific tasks on behalf of users. (*cf. System software.*)

Arithmetic logic unit (**ALU**) The site within a computer where all computations are executed.

Artificial intelligence The use of computers to mimic human intelligence. It includes expert systems and knowledge engineering. There are two main areas of research. The first is an investigation into the nature of knowledge and the use of it in decision making. The second is using the results of the first to develop computer systems capable of demonstrating intelligence so that they may not only make decisions based on their current state of knowledge, but also add to their knowledge bases as a result of their experiences.

Assembler A program which translates instructions written in a specific assembly language into the machine language of a given computer.

Assembly language A computer language of which the syntax comprises mnemonic symbols. It allows a programmer to write programs without having to work in or understand the computer's binary machine language.

Auxiliary storage See *Storage, secondary.*

BASIC An Acronym for Beginners' All-purpose Symbolic Instruction Code. It is a simple high level language.

Batch processing A method of using computer processing in which tasks or data are accumulated over time and input to the computer in a batch.

Binary code A code employing only two symbols. In computing and binary mathematics, these are 0 and 1.

Binary number system A number system having a radix of 2 and whose digits are 0 and 1.

Bit An abbreviation for 'binary digit'. A bit can be of value 0 or 1. It is the fundamental unit of computer storage.

Block An amalgam of computer records, handled for efficiency as one unit for purposes of storage, input and output.

Bubble memory Computer memory, fabricated onto the surface of a wafer of garnet, in which bits are stored as tiny magnetic bubbles. It offers high density storage for random access memory and is non-volatile.

Bug A software error. Also used generally to express any computer system malfunction.

Bulk storage See *Storage, secondary.*

Byte A group of adjacent binary bits operated on as a unit, the size being designated by the computer manufacturer. Latterly a byte has been accepted as comprising eight bits. Thus a 32-bit computer word consists of four bytes and the word of an 8-bit micro consists of a single byte.

Central processing unit (CPU) The 'brain' of a computer; the unit in which processing is carried out. It contains the control unit and the arithmetic logic unit.

Chip A sliver of silicon, or other semiconductor material, into which integrated circuitry is etched. The term is also used to embrace the silicon's protective housing.

COBOL An acronym for COmmon Business-Oriented Language. It is a high level language designed for efficiency in business applications, such as the manipulation of files.

Common mode fault A class of fault which can cause a system failure in a non-stop system – in spite of redundancy. Power failure can be of this type.

Compiler A program for translating a specific high level language into the binary machine language of a particular computer.

Core store Random access memory provided in older computers. It consists of tiny discrete iron cores which can be magnetized in either of two directions, these being used to represent the two possible binary digits.

Cursor An indicator on the screen of a visual display unit which highlights the next character or character position to be operated on. In normal continuous operation it moves automatically on the screen, but it can be manipulated by an operator so as to identify to the computer characters to be deleted or altered, or a position where a character is to be input.

Data 1) Information to be processed, as distinct from information which controls the processing (programs). 2) All information stored by a computer, including program instructions, text, numerics, etc.

Database A collection of files stored as an integrated system. Designed to achieve efficient updating and retrieval of data in specific applications, as well as data consistency, security and minimized redundancy.

Database, hierarchical A database in which the files are structured in a hierarchical manner.

Database, network A database in which any item of data may be linked to any number of other items. The links can form a network (in software) of great complexity, and this type of database is not widely used.

Database, relational A database, modelled on a tabular file structure, in which the files are structured and linked together in accordance with relationships between them.

Database management system (DBMS) A computer program, or system of programs, provided to carry out the operations on a database (e.g. searching, retrieving, updating) efficiently. It allows a user to initiate these operations by the use of a query language based on key words, symbolic names, table headings, etc.

Debugging Eliminating a bug from a computer program or system, i.e. taking corrective action.

Decimal number system The number system in general use. It has a radix of 10 and its digits are the ten familiar figures, 0–9.

Development system See *System, development.*

Disk, magnetic A flat-surfaced disk, formally of metal but latterly also of metal-coated plastic, on whose magnetized surface data is stored in binary form. Data is written to or read from a rotating disk via a magnetic head.

Disk drive The equipment which interfaces disks to a computer. It contains a motor and is precision-engineered to maintain the disk in rotation. It also contains the magnetic heads and other electrical equipment for transmitting data between the disk and the computer.

Down time The time during which a computer system is not in service due to a fault, or for routine maintenance.

Dump, data The transfer of a quantity of data from one storage medium to another – usually from primary to secondary storage.

Dump, security A data dump carried out as a precaution against the data's loss or corruption.

EEPROM Electrically erasable programmable read only memory. A recent development of PROM which can be altered *in situ* by using a prescribed method.

EPROM Erasable programmable read only memory. PROM which can be erased, usually by exposing it to ultra-violet light. It can then be reprogrammed.

Expert system A set of programs written to solve problems or make decisions in a specific field. The usual form is for there to be three programs: a 'knowledge base' which stores information on the subject, an input program which receives information on the problem to be solved, and an 'inference engine' which stores a set of rules for using the knowledge base to solve the defined problem.

External memory See *Storage, secondary.*

Field An area of storage allocated to a single data entity. It may consist of one or more bits, bytes or words.

Fifth generation computer So-called because generations of computer hardware have, to date, comprised valve technology, transistor technology, integrated circuitry, and large or very large scale integrated circuitry. The fifth generation is being researched in Japan, Europe and the USA. Its main features are expected to be artificial intelligence, free communication with users, and parallel processing.

File An organized amalgam of computer records.

Floppy disk A plastic disk coated with a magnetic material on which data may be stored. The secondary storage medium of word processors and most microcomputers.

Flow chart This consists of boxes whose shapes represent their purpose and in which are written statements defining the steps of an algorithm. The linking of the boxes shows the logical paths which may be taken through the algorithm.

FORTRAN An acronym for FORmula TRANslation. It is a

high level language designed to achieve efficiency in scientific and mathematical applications.

Fourth generation languages (**4GLs**) Software packages which constitute 'tools' to allow users to generate high level commands for communication with a computer – usually for a specific application, such as access to a database.

Giga An abbreviation for a hundred million (10^9). Thus five gigabytes (5 Gbytes) equals 5×10^9 bytes.

Graph plotter The physical mechanism which produces graphics in response to signals from a computer.

Graphics Computer output in the form of shapes.

Hardware The tangible equipment which is the material fabric of a computer system. The term embraces the computer, its memory and its peripherals.

Hierarchical database See *Database, hierarchical.*

High level language (**HLL**) A computer programming language whose instructions are close to normal language. It allows a programmer to write programs with a knowledge only of the problem and the language and not of how the computer works or deals with the program. A program in a HLL is translated into a computer's binary machine language by a compiler.

Hot stand-by computer A computer waiting in a state of readiness, with power on, to take over the functions of another computer if the latter should fail.

Housekeeping The operations which are carried out within the computer other than those defined within an applications program. These include storage management within primary and secondary storage and time management in sharing processing resources between programs, inputs from on-line terminals, etc. Housekeeping is mostly performed by the operating system.

Input The entry of data into a computer from a terminal or other external device or from secondary storage.

Input device A device, such as a keyboard, from which data can be read into the computer.

Input-output (**I/O**) **device** A device which can both send data to and receive it from a computer.

Instruction 1) Within a computer an instruction is a set of binary bits, in the computer's machine language, which defines an operation to be performed and the address of the data or the peripheral equipment to be used in the operation. 2) To a high level language programmer, an instruction is a discrete entity of code within a program.

Instruction set The hardware which corresponds to instructions within the computer. The basic functions which a computer is able to execute are wired into its hardware in the form of its instruction set.

Integrated circuit (I/C) An electrical circuit which, instead of being implemented by discrete components wired together, is etched onto the surface of a semiconductor chip.

Interpreter A program which decodes and executes a program, written in a high level language, instruction by instruction. It does not store the object code, so each time the program is to be run it must be interpreted.

Interrupt A signal received by a computer's control unit which causes it to suspend its current operations. Such a signal may occur when an error is detected in the system or when some I/O peripheral device requires attention. The usual course of action is for the interrupt and its cause to be dealt with before control is returned to the point at which it was interrupted.

Joystick A mechanism for controlling the cursor on a screen and by whose movement, in the two horizontal dimensions, graphical information is input to a computer. Its function is similar to that of a mouse.

Key A symbol, such as a name, which identifies a record or other data.

Kilo An abbreviation for a thousand, usually further abbreviated to 'k' or 'K'. When used in the context of primary memory, which is addressed in binary, one kilobyte (Kbyte) equals 1024 bytes. However, disk storage is usually referred to in decimal quantities. To distinguish between the two types of reference, the convention of 'K' for binary (i.e. 1024) and 'k' for decimal (i.e. 1000) is often used.

Knowledge base That part of an expert system which stores a number of items of knowledge on a given subject.

LAN See *Network, local area.*

Language, computer A system of instructions, of defined syntax, designed for communication with a computer.

Large scale integration (LSI) Complex integrated circuitry on a single chip, designated as containing the equivalent of between 10 000 and 100 000 components.

Light pen A device for inputting graphical information to a computer. It is connected to the computer and, when the VDU screen is touched by it, the point of contact is recorded.

LISP An acronym for LISt Processing. A computer language which is based on logical propositions rather than procedures.

Local area network (LAN) See *Network, local area.*

Logical operations The manipulation of data requires a computer to contain circuitry designed to perform logical (Boolean) functions. In electrical terms, these take the form of examining a number of inputs to a device, or gate, and, on the basis of these, making a decision on what form the output should take. The output, as well as each input, is binary and so may have a value of either 0 or 1 at a particular time. Examples of logical functions are AND and OR.

For the AND function there is an output if *all* inputs have a value of 1. Thus a **truth table** for the AND function for two inputs, such that Input 1 AND Input 2 = Output is:

Input 1	*Input 2*	*Output*
0	0	0
0	1	0
1	0	0
1	1	1

For the OR function there is an output if *any* input has a value of 1. Thus a truth table for Input 1 OR Input 2 = Output is:

Input 1	*Input 2*	*Output*
0	0	0
0	1	1
1	0	1
1	1	1

Machine language The set of instructions, for a particular computer, which maps onto that computer's instruction set. A machine language is made up of binary coded instructions and is therefore a low level language. Programs written in assembly or high level language must be translated into a computer's machine language before they can be processed on that computer.

Macro A software instruction or routine, stored in a computer, which enables the computer to carry out a function which is not directly provided within the computer's instruction set. To do this, it makes use of those functions which are wired into the instruction set.

Magnetic core memory See *Core store.*

Mainframe computer A term derived from the huge number of racks which were necessary to house the extensive volume of equipment which comprised the early computers. The 'main' frame(s) supported the central processing unit (CPU). Other racks (or frames) supported the peripheral equipment. Now the term is still used for large computers – particularly in order to distinguish between 'micros', 'minis' and 'mainframes'.

Maintenance, software The correction, improvement, expansion, etc. of software. Indeed, any work carried out on software after it has been made operational.

Man/machine language A language designed for communication between terminal users and computers.

Mega An abbreviation for a million, usually further abbreviated to 'M'.

Memory 1) That part of a computer in which information is stored. 2) Synonymous with 'storage'. See *Storage, primary* and *Storage, secondary.*

Memory address register A register in which the address of the location in memory, which needs to be accessed, is stored in order that addressing can occur.

Microcomputer (micro) A small computer based on semiconductor technology in which the CPU is built on one chip – or very few chips. The small size and low price of microcomputers has allowed the explosion in the ownership and use of computers.

Microprocessor The CPU, usually on a single LSI or VLSI chip, of a microcomputer. Single chip microprocessors are also designed for other dedicated control functions, such as the control of a washing machine's cycle.

Microsecond One millionth of a second.

Millisecond One thousandth of a second.

Minicomputer (mini) A small computer, originally developed on the principles on which mainframes were designed. They are typically powerful and compatible with an extensive range of peripheral devices and also able to use software developed for mainframes. More recently, as microcomputers have become more powerful, minis have been based on micro technology. Thus, the distinction between micros and minis is becoming blurred though, typically, a mini is more expensive, more powerful, and likely to belong to a 'family' or 'range' of compatible, or upward-compatible machines.

Mnemonic A memory jogger, or aid to human memory. It usually takes the form of a symbol which bears some relationship to that which is to be remembered.

Modem MOdulator/DEModulator. A device for translating computer information (which is in digital form) into an analogue form suitable for transmission over analogue communication systems – such as public switched telephone networks (PSTNs) have been to date – and for translating it back at the receiving computer. Modems have been necessary for communication between computers. Currently, however, there are more and more digital networks in existence and, when PSTNs are wholly digital, they will become obsolete.

Mouse A device (sometimes in the shape of a mouse) by which the position of a cursor on a VDU screen can be controlled. It is connected to the computer and its position in a horizontal plane is represented on the screen by the cursor. It is used for the input of graphical information.

Multiprogramming A technique for interleaving the processing of several tasks within the computer. It is normally carried out by the operating system.

Multi-user system A computer system which allows simultaneous inputs from a number of on-line users.

Nano One thousand millionth (10^{-9}). Thus, one nanosecond equals 10^{-9} seconds.

Network database See *Database, network.*

Network, local area (LAN) A homogeneous network for interconnecting computers, usually within a radius of about 5 Km. Transmission is by packets of data, at high speed, usually between 10 and 100 Mbits/sec.

Network, wide area (WAN) A WAN is formed a) when computers or LANs are interconnected over a wider area than could be covered by a single LAN; b) when differing protocols do not allow connection of the various equipments to a single LAN; c) when the interconnecting media, e.g. the PSTN, do not form a homogeneous network.

Non-stop computer system A system designed not to fail as the result of any single fault. This is achieved by hardware redundancy and specially written software. If the design is to be completely successful, the possibility of common mode faults must also have been considered. Non-stop systems are also referred to as 'fault-tolerant' or 'resilient'.

Non-volatile memory Memory whose contents are not destroyed if the power supply is removed. Bubble memory is an example.

Object code The code, in a machine language, into which any program (in source code) must be translated if it is to be processed.

On-line Connected to a computer and under the control of its central processing unit.

Operating system A set of programs which carries out the internal functions and housekeeping of a computer. It forms an interface between a programmer's application programs and a computer's hardware. For a programmer to be abstracted from the hardware, and write programs without a knowledge of how to organize the internal working of a computer, an operating system is essential.

OR, logical See *Logical operations.*

Output 1) To pass data from a computer to a peripheral, such as a printer or display unit, or to secondary storage. 2) The data which is output.

Output device A device, such as a printer or display unit, to which data may be output from a computer.

PABX Private automatic branch exchange. A small telephone exchange, intended for business use, handling from two to several hundred exchange lines on the one hand and from five to several thousand extensions on the other.

Package, software A program, or set of programs, written to perform a particular function and stored on a transportable, non-volatile storage medium. The package market has been increasing in size as the spread of microcomputers has created a demand for software for numerous applications.

Packet A grouping of data, arranged for transmission. A packet consists of a number of fields, such as destination, address, origin, error checking codes, and the data itself.

Packet switching A means of transmitting data, in the form of packets. A message is broken into a number of packets and these are numbered according to their sequence so as to denote their order. They are then dispatched individually into the packet switched network. When they are received at switching points in this network (nodes) they are re-routed according to the occupancy of the network's links, so that packets for the same destination may take different routes to get there. When they finally arrive they are ordered according to their sequence numbers so that the original message is reconstituted. A packet switched network therefore does not allocate dedicated circuits to a 'call', but shares a link between a number of 'calls'.

Parity bit An extra bit, added to the number of bits necessary to encode a character, to enable parity checking.

Parity checking A system of checking data after transmission to ensure that it has retained its integrity in transit. The extra parity bit is set to 0 or 1 so that the total number of bits representing the character sums to an even or odd number, according to whether even parity or odd parity is being used. If a check reveals incorrect parity, retransmission is demanded.

Pascal A high level language named after the French mathematician and philosopher, Blaise Pascal (1623–1662).

PCM See *Pulse code modulation.*

Peer checks Checks made by one programmer of another's work.

Portability (of software) Software which runs on one computer is portable if it can run, without amendment, on another computer.

PL/1 Programming Language 1. A high level language in which the designers attempted to incorporate the features necessary for efficient programming and processing for both mathematical and business applications.

Primary storage See *Storage, primary*.

Processing The performing of operations by a computer. Every instruction must be processed in order to be executed; and every operation requires the processing of one or more instructions, since a computer only functions under the control of software instructions.

Processing, distributed The monitoring, coordination and control of remote processors by a central processor.

Processing, parallel The concurrent processing of two or more tasks.

Processing, real-time The immediate processing of input data so that the results can be output and used within a very short time.

Program The set of instructions, coded in a computer language, which may be stored in a computer's memory and, when subsequently processed, instructs the computer on the performing of a specific task.

Programming, structured A methodical approach to the writing of software which presupposes top/down design and the sub-division of the software into a hierarchical structure of modules. The code of each module is then structured so that its layout is an indication of the operations being executed.

PROLOG An acronym for PROgramming in LOGic. A high level language, based on logical propositions rather than procedures.

PROM Programmable read only memory. Memory which, once written to, may not easily be altered (see also *EPROM* and *EEPROM*).

Protocols, communication The operations, including signalling and the formatting of data, which must be adhered to unvaryingly in order that communication may take place.

PSTN Public switched telephone network.

Pulse code modulation (**PCM**) A process of converting analogue signals into digital form for transmission. Two standards currently exist, in which transmission takes place at 2.048 Mbit/sec and 1.536 Mbit/sec respectively. The former is an international standard; the latter is prevalent in the USA and Japan.

Query language A language by means of which a user gains access to certain software, or a particular process, within a computer, for example a database. The commands in the language are of a high level and are limited to those necessary for the purpose for which the language was designed.

Radix The base of a number system.

RAM Random access memory. Memory which can be accessed directly and within which any location is accessed as easily and quickly as any other. It comprises a computer's main memory or primary storage.

Record A collection of related items of data, each occupying a field and stored together. A number of records constitutes a file.

Redundancy The duplication or replication of a system, or aspects of a system, not due to operational demands but to provide security.

Register A hardware location, usually but not necessarily consisting of a computer word, for the temporary storage of data or instructions when they are about to undergo some operation – such as addressing, processing or output.

Relational database See *Database, relational.*

Response time The delay between the input of a command by a terminal user and the output of a response to it by the computer.

RISC Reduced instruction set computer. A computer whose instruction set comprises only those instructions which are expected to be frequently used.

ROM Read only memory. Memory supplied with software already stored in it and which cannot be altered.

Run-time The time at which a program or process is being processed is the run time of that program or process.

Secondary storage See *Storage, secondary.*

Software The program instructions and data which are, or may be, stored in a computer's memory. In storage, it takes the form of setting the binary storage elements so as to form a coded representation of the instructions or data.

Software based system See *System, software based.*

Software engineering The application of engineering methods and standards to the design, production and testing of software and its documentation so as to achieve software of a higher quality than otherwise.

Software maintenance See *Maintenance, software.*

Source code Program instructions written in a computer language other than machine language, which therefore need to be translated into machine language before they can be processed. (*cf. Object code.*)

Source program A program comprising source code.

Storage The facility with which a computer system is provided for housing the information (instructions and data) necessary for the computer to function and perform tasks. Consists of primary and secondary storage.

Storage, primary The storage provided within the computer itself. It consists of directly addressable random access memory (RAM). Also known as main memory.

Storage, secondary That storage provided externally to the computer, usually on magnetic tape or magnetic disk. Also known as auxiliary storage, bulk storage, and external memory.

Storage, virtual See *Virtual memory.*

Subroutine A set of instructions for carrying out a particular task. Typically, it is 'called' by a main program when that task is required to be executed. The use of subroutines is considered good programming practice as it conforms to the principle of sub-dividing functions into small entities before writing software to execute them.

System, development A computer system on which software development is carried out, even though it may not ultimately be the operational system. (*cf. System, target.*)

System, operating See *Operating system.*

System, software based A system consisting only of a processing machine and a memory. The processing machine is capable of a limited number of simple tasks and the memory is capable of storing software instructions and data. The processing machine processes the data in accordance with the software instructions from the system's own memory and thus functions under the control of the software.

System, target The computer system which will be used in operational circumstances, though software development may be carried out on a development system.

System software Software provided by the computer manufacturer to render the computer system operational and efficient and to provide facilities for the convenience of users. (*cf. Applications software.*)

Systems analyst One who analyses tasks which are proposed for computerization, deduces the resources necessary for performing the computing and data processing tasks, and thus determines the hardware and software components which need to be purchased or developed to achieve a computer system appropriate to perform the tasks.

Throughput The total volume of work achieved by a computer, measured according to defined criteria, within a given time.

Time, access The time taken to retrieve an item of data from a storage location and transfer it to the computer's arithmetic logic unit for processing.

Timesharing The technique of optimizing the use of the central processing unit (CPU) by dividing the time available between a number of tasks. When the tasks include the servicing of terminal users, each user can be given the impression of immediate response and thus the dedicated use of the computer.

Touch-screen A method of inputting graphical information to a computer by touching the screen, the point of contact with the screen being recognized by the computer.

Track A recording path on a magnetic storage medium.

Transmission protocols Rules which must be observed in the transmission of information in order that the information can be routed correctly while in transit and interpreted correctly at the receiving end.

Upward compatibility The ability to transfer the software of one computer in a family or range to a more powerful computer in the same range. This allows the purchase of hardware in the knowledge that, if the system needs to be expanded in the future, the cost and benefits of the software will be safeguarded.

Virtual memory The organization of secondary storage by the operating system so that a programmer need not consider the limitations of the computer's primary storage.

Visual display unit (**VDU**) A screen on which computer output is displayed.

VLSI Very large scale integration. Complex integrated circuitry on a single chip, designated as containing the equivalent of more than 100 000 components.

Volatile memory Memory whose contents are destroyed if the power supply is removed.

Wide area network (**WAN**) See *Network, wide area.*

Winchester disk (**technology**) Magnetic disk technology in which the disk (or disk pack) is within a sealed unit which also contains its own read/write heads.

Word A storage location in computer memory consisting of a number of bits. A word is the entity normally operated on by the central processing unit. The number of bits in a word (the word length) varies between computers, but is typically between eight and 64.

Word processor Microprocessor-based equipment containing software for text processing. It is fast replacing the typewriter in most offices. Typically it uses floppy disks as its storage medium.

INDEX